Acclaim for Anna Deavere Smith's

Letters to a Young Artist

"Thinking of trying to make it as an actor, a writer, a painter, or a singer? Know someone who is, but just doesn't know where to start? This invaluable book points the way. Combining her extraordinary spirit with her tremendous good sense, Anna Deavere Smith has written a nuts-and-bolts guide that is also an anthem to the creative life. It will fire you up throughout your career."
—Jane Wagner and Lily Tomlin

"*Letters to a Young Artist* is a thoughtful and deeply engaging meditation on life and the making of art, written with warmth, humor, and above all, insight and intelligence."
—Glenn Lowry, Director, Museum of Modern Art

"A compelling, inspiring book that takes us on a magical ride through the mind and psyche of any performer or aspiring artist, *Letters to a Young Artist* serves as a powerful compass for unleashing your true potential, awakening a sense of self-mastery, and harnessing the power to create and succeed (and the pictures are great, too!). You've got to read this book."
—Cedric "The Entertainer"

"A treasure. . . . Anna Deavere Smith brilliantly lays out the practical and moral exigencies of an artist's life. . . . This is the book I wish I'd had when I was young and that, as a writer, editor, and teacher, I'm delighted and grateful to have now."
—Dawn Raffel, author of
In the Year of Long Division
and Executive Articles Editor,
O, The Oprah Magazine

"Ring the bell! Class is in session. Anna Deavere Smith's book tells it like it is! . . . With intelligence and passion she gives those who choose a life in the arts some very valuable advice on how to stay on the path. I loved it!"

—Laurence Fishburne, actor

"A very important book—totally engaging, enlightening, and educating. I wish I had had this book when I started photographing in 1963. It would have made my path much clearer and less lonely." —Mary Ellen Mark, photographer

"The brilliant Anna Deavere Smith offers here a practical manual for any artist as well as a powerful reminder of how we can and should live through our art." —Martin Sheen, actor

"Anna Deavere Smith's clear, honest responses to a younger artist's questions offer a philosophical stance on what it is to be an artist. . . . What she has to say is not limited to any age, gender, language, culture, or choice of artistic endeavor."

—Esmeralda Santiago,
author of *When I Was Puerto Rican*

"In *Letters to a Young Artist,* Anna Deavere Smith generously shares her life, her craft, and her heart so that we, the next generation, may become the artists we are meant to be—artists of integrity, courage, resilience, and power."

—Kerry Washington, actor

"It is evident in this timely offering that Anna Deavere Smith has the keen ability not only to listen but also, more importantly, to truly hear. With the grace of generosity shown in *Letters to a Young Artist,* Ms. Smith is endowing a new generation of young artists, compelling them to take that 'leap of faith' toward possibility." —Agnes Gund, President Emerita,
Museum of Modern Art

ANNA DEAVERE SMITH

letters to a young artist

Anna Deavere Smith is an actor, a teacher, a playwright, and the creator of an acclaimed series of one-woman plays based on her interviews with diverse voices from communities in crisis. She has won two Obie Awards, two Tony nominations for her play *Twilight: Los Angeles, 1992*, and a MacArthur Fellowship. She was a Pulitzer Prize finalist for her play *Fires in the Mirror*. She has had roles in the films *Philadelphia*, *The American President*, *The Human Stain*, and *Rent*, and she has worked in television on *The Practice*, *Presidio Med*, and *The West Wing*. The founder and director of the Institute on the Arts and Civic Dialogue, she teaches at New York University and lives in New York City.

Also by Anna Deavere Smith

House Arrest and Piano

Talk to Me: Travels in Media and Politics

Twilight: Los Angeles, 1992

Fires in the Mirror:
Crown Heights, Brooklyn and Other Identities

letters to a young artist

letters to a young artist

ANNA DEAVERE SMITH

ANCHOR BOOKS
A Division of Random House, Inc. • New York

AN ANCHOR BOOKS ORIGINAL, JANUARY 2006

Library of Congress Cataloging-in-Publication Data
Smith, Anna Deavere.
Letters to a young artist / Anna Deavere Smith.
p. cm.
1. Creation (Literary, artistic, etc.)—Miscellanea. 2. Young artists—Conduct of life—Miscellanea. I. Title.
BF411.S58 2006
700'.23—dc22 2005048318

Anchor ISBN-10: 1-4000-3238-5
Anchor ISBN-13: 978-1-4000-3238-9

Book design by Rebecca Aidlin

www.anchorbooks.com

Printed in the United States of America
10 9 8 7 6 5 4 3 2 1

CONTENTS

basics

relationships

work

matters of the mind

matters of the heart

keeping the faith

art and society

the death of cool

letters to a young artist

PREFACE

This book consists of a series of letters to an imaginary young artist whom I've called "BZ." Who is BZ?

If you are an artist of any age, if you are learning the ropes of your art form, and if you want to learn more about the rules of the road in the business of making and selling art, BZ is you.

In my own life as an actress and playwright I have been influenced by many artists, teachers, students, scientists, scholars, and activists; I've been influenced by audiences, and by people whom I never met but only read about in history books. Now I want to pass along to you some of the things I've learned.

I've written this book for the next generation of artists. Art should take what is complex and render it simply. It takes a lot of skill, human understanding, stamina, courage, energy, and heart to do that. It takes, most of all, what a great scholar of artists and educators, Maxine Greene, calls "wide-awakeness" to do that. I am interested in the artist who is awake, or who wants desperately to wake up.

I am writing to you if you are thinking of taking your rightful position as an artist, a position that is both inside and outside of the daily activities of your immediate world. If you read the newspapers, or if you travel and if you talk to people outside your own circle of friends and family, you may be trying to find some kind of a position that allows you to rub up against the very huge and overwhelming world at large. Dare to do it. Great artists have, and they have walked where politicians and lawmakers and even educators wouldn't dare go.

I am addressing you if you are interested in change, in social change, and if you see yourself, potentially, as one of the guardians of the human spirit. In fact, I'm not just addressing you; I am *calling you out*—asking you to make yourself visible. We need you here!

Maybe you are in ninth grade and trying to get a group together to make a musical at your school, or are at a school with no arts program whatsoever, or are in your bedroom with the door shut in a small town somewhere where everyone thinks you're "weird." Maybe you are in a claustrophobic dorm room at college, or in an MFA program feeling kind of low because of the competition after a long day with a disturbing critique. Maybe you've just arrived in New York or LA or Paris or Buenos Aires or Shanghai, one of the many arts capitals of the world, and you just need a way of getting focused or calming down in this new place. I'm writing to you.

And maybe you have the good fortune to go to a private school with a fantastic arts program with everything anyone could possibly need and a really neat chorus director; yes, I would like to talk to you too. Maybe you are in a field someplace looking up at the sky, like the great poet Edna St. Vincent Millay must have been when she wrote her extraordinary poem "Renascence," or maybe you are angry about something that is not fair, the way she must have been when she wrote that bold poem "Conscientious Objector," in which she said, "the password and the plans of our city / are safe with me; never through me Shall you be overcome." I am writing to you.

I'm writing to you if you just plain like to sing—the way my eight-year-old niece does, in the back of her parents' car, as they drive along the Arizona highways under those extraordinary stars, singing in perfect pitch and with an amazing sense of rhythm to anything that happens to be coming out of the sound system. I am writing to you if you love the way the sunset looks wherever you live, and I am writing to you if you are in a housing project somewhere doing the latest dance steps with a group of friends on the breezeway. I am writing to you if you are far enough along that you are already making art somewhere, like my friend the painter Ellen Gallagher, who told me she went to Africa and plopped herself down in the middle of the road and started drawing and attracted a crowd. And I am writing to you if you would like to go to Africa or southern Asia or Latin America or to a rural town on the Mississippi Delta, or anywhere in the world where you think you could use your art to draw people together and to make a difference in their lives.

When I put this book together, I decided to arrange the letters not chronologically but more or less according to certain topics that tend to emerge when artists "talk shop" to one another. In the case of most artists, of course, talking shop also means talking goals, dreams, philosophies, ideals.

I know that dreams motivate us. But I believe it is your vision, as well as your dreams, that will make you an artist, perhaps even a great artist. Cornel West, another scholar, told me eloquently that hope calls for a leap of faith that goes "beyond the evidence to create new possibilities based on visions that become contagious." These visions, he says, allow people to engage in "heroic actions, always against the odds, no guarantee whatsoever." People who run schools and cities and institutions don't want to bank on art because there's no guarantee that it will help make test scores, or anything else, any better. Sometimes I think they don't want to bank on art because there's never any guarantee that it will sell. But if you are like me, you are drawn to the idea of the seer who makes visions that become contagious: visions that allow people to engage in heroic actions. It's the *allowing* that art makes possible. We traditionally think that it's the patron who gives the artist an allowance. Yet it's the artist who gives *society* a large allowance. The artist gives us the allowance to imagine things another way.

I was trained at a time when artists were thought to be "special" people. I don't think we are so special. I think the world around us is incredibly special, incredibly magnificent, in its lightest and darkest and most ordinary muted parts. I am looking to speak, in this book, to you brave folk, younger than I, who are trying to express something that you feel will make a difference in the way this earth stays in orbit. I am trying to make a call, with this book, to you young brave hearts who would like to find new collaborations with scholars, with businesspeople, with human rights workers, with scientists, and more, to make art that seeks to study and inform the human condition: art that is meaningful.

Anna Deavere Smith
Montauk, New York
2005

INTRODUCTION

Dear BZ:

Let me introduce myself to you. My name is Anna Deavere Smith. I guess you heard that you won me in an auction. For better or for worse.

I have agreed to mentor you for a period of five years. Somebody you know (have I got it right that it was your grandmother?) made the highest bid on me as an item at a charity fund-raiser. My deal was that I would mentor whoever "won" me at the auction in some way for the next five years. This is new for me. I've never been auctioned before. (My ancestors were.)

They told you I'm an actress and a playwright. I make one-woman shows in which I play up to fifty characters in an evening. I interview people with a tape recorder and use their verbatim words to make these plays. It'll all make sense the more I write to you. In fact, I'll include little excerpts of those interviews from time to time. And I hope someday you can see my work.

I am intimidated by the charge of "mentoring" you. I understand that you are "into painting"? I don't know a thing about painting! There are many great paintings that I like, Rufino Tamayo's *The Comedians*, or Picasso's *Guernica*, to name two. And I've just seen some gorgeous watercolors by a British artist named Chris Ofili. Do you know him? Ellen Gallagher: Do you know her? And then I just saw some work of Sigmar Polke. Anyway, I suppose I'm grasping at straws, because as I say I know nothing about painting. I see it as one of the highest art forms, and one of the most ambitious.

I hope that some of what I know from being a writer and an actress can translate to what you do. Feel free to share my letters with others around you. I heard that you hang in an "arts crowd"? Are they dancers, poets, slam poets, hip-hop artists, cellists? Send details! All I know about you so far is that you are a teenager in an urban high school in Denver. And I gather your grandmother is concerned because they have no arts program there at the moment. Anyway, please tell me as much as you would like about yourself.

Looking forward,

ADS
San Francisco
August 1999

basics

Presence

Dear BZ:

Presence. You want to know what it is. Well, you hit on my favorite subject.

First of all, even before I became an actress I was told I had "presence." "Stage presence." I didn't know what that meant. I forgot about it. Long after I had trained to become an actress, I came upon the word in a way that was intriguing to me.

Joseph Chaikin was a theater director who came to prominence in the sixties in the experimental theater scene in New York. He wrote a book called *The Presence of the Actor*. In it he defines presence in this way: "a kind of deep libidinal surrender which the performer reserves for his anonymous audience." He then went on to write that sometimes a person has "presence" onstage, but not in life. And then he wrote: "Gloria Foster has presence."

At the time I did not know who Gloria Foster was. She is in two *Matrix* movies; she played the Oracle. As soon as I had a chance to see her perform, I did. She was extraordinary. And the interesting thing about Gloria Foster was that in person, she was not at all a "close to you" kind of a woman. By the time I met her I met a woman who definitely kept her own space. Onstage it seemed that the light shone right through her, and that, in fact, the light found her wherever she was onstage. Her film work was filled with both dignity and humanity. Her death left a hole in the theater.

I agree that presence is that feeling that the person onstage or in a film is standing right next to you. In film the presence blasts across the screen. Presence defies the limits of a person's body, defies the limits of the actual space it takes up.

Some people call presence charisma. Perhaps it's the same thing. There are many charismatic people who are not artists. And presence is not the same as fame, by the way.

If you think about the people around you, there are many who have presence. There's a woman who is a cashier at Wilkes Bashford, a clothing store in San Francisco. Her name is "Miss Kish"—that's a nickname she has been given. For years I went into that store and was intimidated by Miss Kish. She is an African-American woman in a store that's mostly frequented by whites (with the exception of a few famous blacks like the former mayor of San Francisco, Willie Brown). She wore a man's hat at the cash register, often a bright red one. She looked as though she did not suffer fools. I was shocked to get a phone call from Miss Kish in November 2004, when John Kerry lost to George Bush. She wanted to know my opinion. To me, it was as if Kerry had called!

Presence means you hold your own space, control the space around you, and sometimes welcome others into it.

I saw a man in New York City in the late seventies kissing trees on a regular basis. Of course, such an action is bound to attract attention, but presence is not merely the attraction of attention. When he kissed a tree, it took my breath away. He was an older man with white hair. It was his level of commitment that gave him presence.

Lauren Hutton, the first supermodel, was discovered in the sixties by Diana Vreeland, the editor of *Vogue* magazine. At the very moment that Diana Vreeland discovered Lauren,

Lauren did not realize she was attracting attention. She was in Vreeland's office as a model who simply showed the clothes to Vreeland and others at *Vogue* who made decisions about fashion. She was too short to be a high-fashion model. She was stunned by the scene in Vreeland's office—the glamour, the diversity of looks and attitudes. She actually stopped working and sat on a windowsill to watch the action, while all the other models paraded in and out for the staff of *Vogue*. Vreeland suddenly pointed to Lauren with her long white glove—a glove she wore to turn the many pages of images she had to look at—and said, "And *you* have quite a presence." Lauren actually looked out the window, thinking that Vreeland was talking about somebody behind her. "*You*, you stay after," said Vreeland. And a multimillion-dollar career was launched, and nineteen covers of *Vogue* magazine. Her presence was the *intensity of her gaze*—not the expectation that others *would be gazing at her*.

Lauren also has presence of *wit*. Presence of *mind*. I joked with her: "I think you should have a Kennedy Center Honor for your smile."

"Oh, you do, do you?" she said in her Southern accent.

"Yeah, we live in a culture infatuated with beauty—I mean, singers get the Kennedy Center Honor, writers get it, comics get it; why don't beautiful people get it? Our whole culture is based on beauty, and you have quite a smile. It should be honored."

"Is that right?" she said, clearly getting a kick out of this exchange.

"Yes, I think I'll write George Bush a letter."

"Will you sign your name?" she asked.

"Of course," I said.

Memphis Smith, my dog. Here, presence is on display in part because of the photographer, Mary Ellen Mark. She turns a sigh into a laugh.

"All three of 'em?" she asked.

Presence means paying attention to find any opportunity to engage.

My dog has presence. Her name is Memphis. In Los Angeles people stop their cars and shout out the window, "What kind of dog is that?" In New York, people stop me on the street to talk to her. Once, when she was a puppy, she slipped out of her collar at a busy intersection in New York. I threw myself on top of her. People ran from all corners. "Is your dog having an epileptic fit? Wanna use my cell phone?" I even thought to myself on that occasion that they'd probably let a human being just lie out on the street, but people ran from all corners to help a dog. Haydee, who is from Peru, sometimes walks Memphis for me when I'm working. She told me, "Anna, everybody wanna talk to Memphis; they don't see me; they only see Memphis." With me on the elevator in my building was a woman—a stockbroker type, in her own thoughts, at the end of a long day, tired. We were riding in silence. (I live in a building that's not so large. Nonetheless, people keep their personal "space" in the elevator.) Suddenly she lit up and said to me, "Is Memphis your dog?" I was startled by the suddenness of her question and the life that came out of an otherwise day-drained persona.

"Yes," I said.

"That dog makes my day!" she said.

Same scene in an elevator in Los Angeles. In LA Memphis was not allowed in the main elevator—she had to take the service elevator. My assistant hated the service elevator; she said it "smelled." Memphis loved the service elevator—the smells of the men, the smells of their lunch, pizza, etc., the smells of their bodies, the smells of work. She's a work dog after all, part Australian cattle dog—a herder. One day I was on the main elevator—without Memphis, of course. A man who had been pointed out to me as an archconservative turned to me and said, "That dog of yours is fantastic."

"She's a mutt," I said.

"Well, she's got some border collie in her. Great dog. Very *alert*," he pronounced.

"Thanks," I said. And he strutted out of the elevator, crossed the lobby, and climbed into his SUV.

Alert. Part of presence is about being *alert.*

I asked a friend of mine, "Why does everybody look at Memphis?"

"Because she's pretty," my friend said simply.

But presence is not just about being pretty. Presence is your ability to be present. Because Memphis is part Australian cattle dog—a red heeler—she is very intense, and does not like to miss a beat. She pays attention to the movings and goings-on around her. "Pretty" does help. But "pretty" is not the same as presence.

If two people have an argument, Memphis runs back and forth between the two of them, as if she is afraid they will leave the room. As a herder, she is looking for every opportunity to keep moving things together. Presence is having something that you are wired to do, that you are committed to do, so committed to do it that it's almost like it's in your DNA. It's being ready at all times and looking for every possible opportunity.

Presence is not so easy. There is so much *stuff* out there. To get presence, you have to move through layers and layers of commotion and noise and other sites that grab the light. It's hard to grab the light these days. People used to talk about Andy Warhol's fifteen minutes of fame. Now it's more like one minute.

It might seem that presence is all about advertising. You might think, just hire a good PR firm. PR is powerful, but it's not the same as presence. Real presence has to come from the inside.

Real presence is the feeling that the person onstage is right next to you *because you long to have them there. Or because you are terrified that they could come after you and get you in your seat.* Monsters have presence. Godzilla had presence. Terrorists have presence. Osama bin Laden has presence.

Presence doesn't have to do with likability. Nor does being a provocateur guarantee presence.

Often people who have presence know that *you* are there before you know *they* are there. Israel, one of the doormen in my building, was beside himself. Israel is Puerto Rican. It was winter. What had just happened? "I seen J. Lo. On the street!" he whispered. "And I seen her and she just went like this." And he put his finger to his lips, "Sssh." He was practically blushing. "I said, 'Cool. Cool.' And she just walked on by; I was like, 'I got you covered. Cool,'" he said. His eyes were twinkling. "That woman," he said emphatically. "There needs to be a picture of her in the dictionary beside the words 'Latin woman'!"

Presence can be magical. It can delight the people around you. Think of when you were a kid, and you had a favorite friend, or a favorite relative—something enchanted you—presence is *enchanting*. And it does not always have to do with what a person *actually* is. It is what you *wish* they were. There is myth in presence. This works for that which we wish to embrace us, and it is the same for that which we fear. There is also magic in fear.

Jacob Lawrence, the great African-American painter, moved as a child from Atlantic City to Easton, Pennsylvania, to Philadelphia to Harlem, where he settled with his mother when he was thirteen. He did not often see white people until he became famous as a painter and was embraced by the mainstream art world. His parents had grown up in the South, where people were lynched. He believed that all white people were potential lynchers—and so he was always alert to

One of Jacob Lawrence's paintings from his sixty-panel *Migration Series,* which depicts the journey that members of his family and other African Americans made from the South to the North in the early part of the twentieth century. This painting (panel #15) is a representation of a lynching.

the possibility that one of them could appear. Especially if one showed up in Harlem, where he otherwise felt safe, at home, surrounded by his own.

"If I saw a white man," he told me, "I would automatically think, Oh, that's a lyncher."

So I asked him, "Well, what happened when you got famous and you were around white people?"

"Oh, you know," he said calmly, and with a tone of reassurance, "these things are all fears, like children are afraid of ghosts, and goblins, and eventually they go away."

But for the time that the fearsome object has its hold on you, it has presence. *Presence is having a hold on the desires and fears of those around you.*

If you have presence, it could be helpful to know how to use it.

Study photographs to learn about presence.

There is a photograph of Naomi Campbell taken at the Cuban National Ballet School, by Patrick Demarchelier. She is poised to dance with a male dancer. Her focus is direct, her concentration razor-sharp.

Naomi Campbell has presence.

President Bill Clinton has presence. He is known for remembering the names of people he's met only once, and remembering details of conversations.

Presence requires being aware. Presence requires paying attention. Presence requires using your intelligence. Presence requires allowing *others* to make an impact on you. This means putting your mind on them, not just on yourself.

Presence is empathy. Cesar Chavez had presence. He understood the plight of the migrant workers and was able to speak *to them and for them.*

Presence can come from deep commitments to beliefs, unpopular beliefs.

I saw a photograph of the Queen Mother, standing simply in a garden with her purse. Now she had presence.

Presence is not the same as attracting attention. It's not a gimmick. It is not a brand. I said previously that presence was about "grabbing the light." No. It's about *finding* the light and being a part of it. These days, I believe that light might just be *in* the audience, *with* the public, *in* the world, *among* the possibilities of "us" human beings rather than in the language of "self."

Oprah Winfrey has presence. Big time!

It is harder and harder to have presence in a world of so much noise, so much show, so much amplification.

Naomi Campbell in a fashion photograph taken in the School for the Ballet Nacional in Havana, Cuba. The photograph was taken by Patrick Demarchelier for *Harper's Bazaar.* Notice Campbell's focused gaze and that of the dancer.

Presence will probably, in the near future, be based on absolute authenticity. Whoever can achieve that in a world of brands, and seductions, and false promises, and addictions to false loves, will be truly charismatic.

I'm sure you have presence, BZ. Expand it. Dare to open your heart to the good and bad around you.

ADS

P.S. I am writing this to you on the back of several napkins in a restaurant in Tiburon, California. My hosts are very late. A

Sri Lankan busboy just walked by and said, "You must have a lot on your mind. You are writing a *lot.*" (He laughed out loud.) Gosh, I just realized my pen leaked! I have ink all over my hand! No matter. This has got to be one of the most beautiful spots in the world. It's just after sunset, and I can see the Golden Gate Bridge lighting up in the distance. A ship just went by with black sails and a string of lights. It reminded me of *Othello*. I'll be writing from all sorts of places. I'm a gypsy—which goes with the territory. So sometimes the spots will be glamorous, and sometimes I'll be writing to you from the back of a rental car. It's not all a vase of roses, this life! Hope to meet you soon.

Being In It, and Out of It, at the Same Time

Dear BZ:

Being "in it, and out of it, at the same time" is a sort of fundamental first exercise one should do as one develops as an artist.

Did you take ballet when you were younger, or do you now? You know how in the beginning of the class you go through all the positions in the warm-up, and the positions become the foundation or the basis of the ballet? It's a basic vocabulary. Like when you bake, you need flour, butter, sugar, some kind of liquid, etc. The fundamental ingredients.

Well, I believe that fundamental to becoming an artist is understanding the *position* of an artist, rehearsing that position, and practicing that position. It is from that position that you will develop an eye, an ear, and a heart. These three organs are essential. Yes, as a painter you will need a hand, and as an actor I need a voice and a body—but before getting to those, we need to develop the eye, the ear, the heart.

We do that by learning how to step outside of given situations to watch, to listen, and to feel, and to feel *as* others as much as to feel things *about* others. Feeling as others is empathy. Feeling *for* others is sympathy. Empathy is more useful and more important. It requires more rigor. That rigor will make you stronger of heart and spirit. Empathy requires a very highly developed imagination. It is more active than sympathy. It requires more intellectual development. Sympathy, to me, is just tears. Empathy is potentially very productive.

Stepping outside gives you the space to watch, listen, feel. To step outside you must suspend opinions and judgments. It doesn't mean that you are devoid of them. It means that you can control them long enough to watch, listen, and feel. You store what you have learned, and then you do what you will with what you have gathered. You may even try to influence how others watch, listen, and feel. But first and foremost you must be able to step outside.

Read an essay by Bertolt Brecht, the mid-twentieth-century German playwright, called "Street Scene." In it he describes an accident scene, where people come out into the street and describe an accident. They all give their version. He calls the telling—the storytelling that happens—a kind of "natural theater." It will remind you that you have to be available to watch and listen and feel for all scenes.

To me, artists are students of the human condition, poten-  tially. Being outside does not mean being without compassion. But it does mean that you may sometimes become clinical.

Years ago I interviewed the head of pediatric surgery at Sloan-Kettering hospital in New York. I asked him what had moved him to become a cancer surgeon for children. I thought he would tell me a moving story about having seen a child suffering, but instead he replied, "I wanted to do bigger operations."

What was driving him was his desire to be a very good surgeon, and to discover things. I think as artists we too should want to do "bigger operations."

Standing in and out at the same time is a structural matter.

It is a way of bringing order to the otherwise chaotic situation of life. I say chaotic because as an artist you are both *in* life and *commenting on* life. That's your position.

ADS
New York City
February 2000

Confidence

Dear BZ:

You asked me about confidence. How to work on confidence.

It's coincidental that you should bring this up. I'm in Gooding, Idaho, going to rodeos with Brent Williams, who is a bull rider. The goal of a bull rider is to stay on a bucking bull for eight seconds. He is then evaluated by how well he rode. He needs a good animal for that. By good I mean not an easy animal but one that gives a rough ride. The bull rider is evaluated on the *roughness of the ride* and how he deals with it.

I like the way Brent talks about confidence—choosing to value determination over confidence. I agree with him. Confidence is a static state. Determination is active. Determination allows for doubt and for humility—both of which are critical in the world today. There is so much that we don't know, and so much that we know we don't know. To be overly confident or without doubt seems silly to me.

Determination, on the other hand, is a commitment to win, a commitment to fight the good fight. The bull rider says it better than I. There's a poetry to his language, so I'm going to reproduce it just that way:

CONFIDENCE

Confidence is a big part of it—
But I think I ride more off of determination than confidence.
Confidence is you've been on that bull before and you know
you're gonna ride 'im.

Brent Williams, a bull rider from Shoshone, Idaho, whom I perform as a character in my shows. I like his ideas about determination.

Confidence is—
Kind of like—maybe bein' cocky about it.
But in a good way.

If you ride with determination—

"(Forget) the form, get the horn."

Tuff Hedeman said that.
He's in the movie *8 Seconds*.
And you know he was the world champion like three times—
'Cause he didn't ride with style; he rode with determination.
Just hang on till the whistle blows—
No matter if you're ridin' upside down.
Determination.
Like Pat, my wife's uncle,
He always said, "Man,
you got the most try than any kid I have ever seen."
Try and determination is the same thing.
And you know, like—
There've been a lot of times that—
There's a lot of bull riders,
They safety up—
And me, I've never safetied up my whole life.
And a lot of times it may get me stepped on or something—
You're just gonna ride till your head hits the back of the dirt.

BZ, the point is, you may not need confidence (which comes with time) as much as you need your personal determination to hang in there no matter what.

ADS
Gooding, Idaho
August 2003

Self-Esteem

Dear BZ:

Those are good and important questions about self-esteem. It's a lot like confidence. Although there's something about the term "self-esteem" that's more clinical, as if it comes out of psychotherapies. Right? Like, educators might say that poor children who grow up without parental guidance or involvement in their educations lack "self-esteem." They'd say that before they'd say they lack "confidence." Perhaps confidence is an offshoot of self-esteem. Self-esteem refers to your general state of well-being, the way you think about yourself.

It's a good subject for us to look at because, in the arts, value, as we have discussed, is like a yo-yo. You can't base your self-esteem on how well your work is selling or on how well it's received. We live in business; we live in commerce. It's the air we breathe.

But let's take commerce out of it. What if you did a painting just for your family and unveiled it at a family holiday? There might be one person or two people who would "get" what you are doing. Others might see it as "weird" or simply "artistic" (whatever that means). The nineteenth-century Russian playwright Anton Chekhov's great play *The Seagull* captures this perfectly in one of the opening scenes. A young man, Kostya, is putting on a play. It's an innovative play. (It isn't ever clear whether it's a good play.) He casts a girl whom he loves in the play. She seems distracted. He presents the play for his mother, a famous actress, who is visiting the country estate where he lives with his aging uncle. His mother is accompanied by her lover, who is a famous writer. Everything goes wrong. It's a catastrophe, and he is beside himself. A family friend, Dr. Dorn, approaches him when all the audience has left and says, "I liked your play." What he meant was—he understood what Kostya was trying to do.

Robert Brustein, critic and former head of the American Repertory Theater in Cambridge, Massachusetts, said to me once that we all need a Dr. Dorn. If you unveiled a painting at a family gathering, and a cousin or a brother got more attention for doing a backflip at that very moment, or if something went awry—if a relative mocked your work, or people went on to chat about mundane things—you could end up feeling pretty bad. And who knows? Years later, that might be considered a great painting. (To this day certain people call my work "*skits*"!)

So self-esteem is that which gives us a feeling of well-being, a feeling that everything's going to be all right—that we can determine our own course and that we can travel that course. It's not that we travel the course alone, but we need the feeling of agency—that if everything were to fall apart, we could find a way to put things back together again. And hopefully we'd never get to that, because we would have watched out for hazards.

Part of self-esteem is resourcefulness. I am always amazed to learn stories of people who have built businesses, and they've collapsed and they've built new ones. The stories of immigrant cultures are full of resourcefulness. But if someone lacked self-esteem, he or she would not be resourceful.

The Slanted Door Restaurant in San Francisco became well-known very quickly. I once called 411 to get the phone number. The operator said, "Oh, that's a great place." On another occasion, coming home from the airport, I was going directly there, and the cabdriver said, "I take a lot of people there." Word of mouth was building an audience for this place. It was run by a Vietnamese family. Because they had found a way to present traditional food in a kind of hip atmosphere, I was intrigued by them. I began to talk to the owner and learned his story over time. He and his family had been what was known as "boat people." They'd made their way to the United States, and with basically nothing, managed to start a clothing business. It made money but then failed. They then started the restaurant, which is a huge success in San Francisco—a major part of the culture of the city. Whenever I hear such stories, I have one big unanswered question—what gives people the basic solid foundation to know that they can "do" it?

Maybe that's not the question. Some people seem to be able to organize themselves around big ideas, and others cannot. This has to do with self-esteem. Self-esteem for creative people is important inasmuch as it is a part of what helps you organize yourself and others around an idea, so that it can come to fruition. Ideas are a dime a dozen; to make them real takes consistent, persistent application of energy toward that idea. Self-esteem is a foundation. And yet, there are many successful people who would seem to have low self-esteem. If you have a healthy amount of self-esteem, it is one more tool needed to help you do things that are ambitious and sometimes difficult.

When I was a girl, the old ladies in my church would drone out a song that went:

On Christ the solid
Rock I stand.
All other ground is sinking sand.

And the verses go on to spell out how you can't count on friends or other earthly matters to get you through, but Christ will. Sometimes they would stomp and clap a little when they sang this song—and the way it echoed inside of the church with its wooden floors and stone walls gave me the feeling of the very solid rock they were describing. I chose that song as one of the songs to be sung at my mother's funeral.

An American psychotherapist or psychiatrist would tell you that self-esteem is built by your parents, by your upbringing, by experiences in your childhood. I don't think that this conclusion exists in every culture. Some cultures are more spiritual than ours. Some cultures have ways of creating that feeling of well-being—and for some people it is spiritual. In acting school, I found that Transcendental Meditation, as well as prayer, helped me get through hard times. Meditation and prayer also caused me to shut everything down (twice a day) and learn more about my own resourcefulness. Our acting conservatory had a meditation room. And it was also down the hill from a large cathedral. Without the meditation room and the cathedral I would have probably been on sinking sand.

Experiences from the outside, and the way you integrate yourself with the outside, can lead you to gain a more confident stride. One thing is for sure: Self-esteem cannot really be built from the outside. You begin to see the real evidence that you can, in fact, affect the things around you. These experiences ultimately integrate themselves inside—if that foundation is there. Self-esteem does not come from surrounding yourself with people and things that seem to increase your value. Real self-esteem is an integration of an inner value with things in the world around you.

It's about your worth. Your self-worth. And as we have discussed throughout our correspondence, you—and only you—can ultimately put the price tag on that. Your tag reveals not only how you value yourself, but how imaginative and original you are about valuing others. In my experience, happier people are people who have not only a high price tag on themselves, but a high price tag on the people around them—and the tags don't necessarily have to do with market value. They have to do with all the sense that adds up to human value.

Be strong, be new, be you.

Anna

Discipline

Dear BZ:

Discipline—both mental and physical—is crucial.

Melvin van Peebles is a black filmmaker who hit the scene in the seventies with a movie called *Sweet Sweetback's Badasssss Song*, an independent film that made a big splash. He made a lot of money and made a place for himself on the cultural landscape. His son, Mario van Peebles, has now made a film that is based on his father's film. Last night I hosted, along with others, a screening of Mario's film. Melvin van Peebles, of course, was there. He must be in his mid-sixties, and he is in perfect physical shape. He was standing by the bar, and I asked him not about the film but about his physique.

"You look like you work out," I said.

"Every day," he said.

People who actually work out every single day have no problem talking about it. He and I agreed that we have to get up and go immediately to the gym, the pool, wherever our workout is, without doing anything before.

"If I get up and think, 'Let me have a cup of coffee first,' it ain't happ'nin'," he said.

Not even a cup of coffee. I'm the same way. If I go to the computer or take a newspaper before heading to the gym, there's a chance I won't get there.

Last Saturday night I met a man in his forties who looked

to be in his thirties. He lives in California, and works out constantly—running, riding his bike, rowing on an inside rowing machine. I brought up the story about Melvin van Peebles and he agreed. He told me that he'll be sitting on his couch at ten P.M. and start to doze. He'll make himself get up, put on his running shoes, and go out for a run at that hour. That's his second or third workout for the day.

You could say that these people are "obsessed." But I tell the two stories to get to the subject of discipline.

The life of an artist is not a state of "being." It even sounds pretentious, sometimes, to call oneself blanketly "an artist." It's not up to you or me to give ourselves that title. A doctor becomes a doctor because he or she is formally given an MD. A scholar in the university is formally given a PhD, a counselor an LLD, a hairstylist a license, and so forth.

We are on the fringe, and we don't get such licenses. There are prizes and rewards, popularity and good or bad press. But you have to be your own judge. That, in and of itself, takes discipline, and clarity, and objectivity. Given the fact that we are not "credentialed" by any institution that even pretends to be objective, it is harder to make our guild. True, some schools and universities give a degree for a course of study. But that's a business transaction and ultimately not enough to make you an "artist."

I suppose one way of evaluating your credentials has to do with how much work you are able to get; yet it's not so simple. It's not even necessarily true that if people trust you and have confidence that you will deliver, they will hire you.

Part of earning that title "artist" is the quality of your interaction with others: how much you manage, as I said about presence, to activate the desires and fears of others through—and here's a new idea—the use of metaphors and fictions. This does not require fame and fortune. You can do this in your family, at your school, at your church, in your community.

We who work in the arts are at the risk of being in a popularity contest rather than a profession. If that fact causes you despair, you should probably pick another profession. Your desire to communicate must be bigger than your relationship to these chaotic and unfair realities. Ideally, we must be even more "professional" than lawyers, doctors, accountants, hairdressers. We have to create our own standards of discipline.

All of the successful artists I know are very disciplined and very organized. Even if they don't look organized, they have their own order.

I interviewed the printmaker and sculptor Kiki Smith, who is considered one of the finest printmakers of her generation. She has a house on New York's Lower East Side. The place was a cacophony of activity. Hammers were going, assistants were coming in and out, stuff was all over the dining room table. She travels nonstop. She goes to museums nonstop. I asked her curator how she gets so much done. The curator told me that she never stops moving her hands. That is, she's always making something. During the interview she was making a large clay cat sculpture. It was true: Throughout our entire discussion, she never stopped moving her hands. Her hands are evidence of that—the muscles, the flexibility, the form of her fingers.

What we become—what we *are*—ultimately consists of what we have been doing—what we eat, what we drink, how we have been moving.

In 1974 I started swimming. I will never forget the first day I went to the pool and had decided to make swimming a part of my everyday regimen. Swimming was the perfect exercise; either you sink or you swim. Soon after, I understood something about acting that I would take with me to rehearsals with my classmates: "Talking about acting is like thinking about swimming."

Discipline is different for every artist. Regina Carter, a very disciplined jazz violinist and composer, nonetheless once jokingly remarked: "I'm getting ready to get ready." Joshua Redmond, the saxophonist, also comes to mind. In a meeting I had with him, I noticed that if there was a lull in the conversation, he was moving his tongue against his teeth, making the plosive noises of songs he was thinking about.

Judith Jamison: another disciplined person. Artistic director of the Alvin Ailey American Dance Theater, she was at one time a major modern dance star. When I interviewed her, she was on time, prepared, and on to the next thing. Speaking of her talent, what she would call her gift as a dancer, she said, "This gift, and I believe it's a gift; if I forget it's a gift it will go away." (She said this with a specific kind of upward inflection, not so as to ask a question, but as a soft challenge or offering, which comes from confidence, not lack of certainty.)

Be more than ready. Be present in your discipline. Remember your gift. Be grateful for your gift and treat it like a gift. Cherish it, take care of it, and pass it on. Use your time to bathe yourself in that gift. Move your hand across the canvas. Go to museums. Make this into an obsession.

I once asked M. Thomas Shaw, the Episcopal bishop of Massachusetts, what it was like to meet the Pope. He said, "It was obvious to me by his presence that he was a man who prayed."

What you are will show, ultimately. Start now, every day, becoming, in your actions, your regular actions, what you would like to become in the bigger scheme of things.

ADS
New York City
April 2004

The Man

Dear BZ:

"The Man." We have to reckon with the Man, regardless of what shape he comes in.

I thought about this today while having lunch with my friend Paul Costello. Paul, who worked for first lady Rosalynn Carter when Jimmy Carter was president of the United States, has spent a lot of his life in Washington. His wife is a political reporter. He understands a lot about power from watching how it works up close. He reads several newspapers daily, observing the effects of what people say and do.

We were sitting by the sea at the Hotel Halekulani in Honolulu, which was built in the nineteenth century. We talked at length about his career and mine. (It's important to have friends whose careers differ from yours and to learn what you can from their struggles, and vice versa.) I talked about how, in my career, there were black men who were more or less the "gatekeepers" of my fate. Or so I thought.

You may look at me and just see me as a woman who has certain accomplishments from paving my own way. The fact is, we all work in large, complicated communities. In my case, some of the men who grew up in my generation—black men—seem to play the role of the go-between between white people in power and artists like myself who are not a part of traditional institutional structures. There are two black men in particular who have a lot of power in each of the realms in which I move. For this reason, I sometimes have the feeling that without their "go-ahead" to whites making decisions, I can't move. In all honesty, I don't know if my feeling is the reality. I was feeling that way while I was visiting with Paul. He put down his glass of iced tea, wiped his mouth with his cloth napkin, and said very simply: "They are the Man."

"The what?" I asked.

"The *Man*," he said. "They may be your friends, but they are also the Man. They work for the Man." He paused for a moment. "And they are the *Man*." He paused for another moment and said succinctly, "You're not the Man. You wouldn't be good at it." He paused again and said passionately, raising his voice to make the point, "You *wouldn't want* to be the Man!"

Paul took another sip of his iced tea and looked at me out of the corner of his eye to see how I reacted.

I stared out at one of the boats in the gorgeous sea in this exquisite setting.

I thought to myself, Well, he's right. My job in my work is not to *acquire* power; it's to *question* power. What I say I believe is that my job is to see the world upside down, to doubt, to question, to ask. I hope I believe what I say I believe.

Let me tell you something, BZ—a lot of times you take a trip halfway around the world. You think the trip is for one thing (in this case Paul had invited me to speak at the University of Hawaii, where he currently works), and you come away with something else. You change in a way you did not expect. These are the lessons that come well after school, college, training, and apprenticeships. These lessons are not full courses; they are two sentences long. I felt I had gotten a minidegree in two minutes.

"The Man." We have to reckon with the Man.

I first heard the expression in the sixties while watching Lorraine Hansberry's play *A Raisin in the Sun* in its movie version starring Sidney Poitier, sitting with my entire family as it played out on black-and-white TV:

MAMA: Where you been, son?

WALTER: (*Breathing hard*) Made a call.

MAMA: To whom, son?

WALTER: To the Man. (*He heads for his room*)

MAMA: What man, baby?

WALTER: (*Stops in the door*) The Man, Mama. Don't you know who the Man is?

RUTH: Walter Lee?

WALTER: *The Man*. Like the guys in the streets say—the Man. Captain Boss—Mistuh Charley . . . Old Cap'n Please Mr. Bossman . . .

In the black power movement, "the Man" was an expression that connoted the white man. It started as "the white man this, the white man that"—meaning a man in power. It got shortened to "the Man." Now anybody could be the Man.

You will always have to deal with the Man. Unless you are the Man. But even the president of the United States—currently the "leader" of the "free world," the "leader" of the only superpower in the world—can have his hands tied by other forces. In the terrorist world, for example, there is the Man—and we don't even know who it is.

It is crucial for you to know who the Man is in any situation in which you find yourself. And to know what your relationship to the Man is, and how you would get to the Man if you needed to. Often there is a route you have to take to get to the Man. It's not always obvious. So on the first day of any situation, learn who the Man is and what the route to the Man is. Sometimes the most unassuming person is closest to the Man. And you *never know* what kinds of relationships the Man has or who has his or her ear.

I nodded to Paul. I realized I had to reckon with what Paul had said. That these two black men wore two hats with me—one was they were my friends; the other was they were each the Man.

The Man is whoever has the money or whoever has the power to work out the money needed and the venue needed to expose your art. This person, or group of persons, owns the studio, or runs the studio, or runs the theater, or runs the concert hall. This person decides who gets the grants; edits or owns the newspapers that write about your work; owns the magazines, or edits the magazines, or edits the photographs that go into the magazine that you might be in someday with an article about you and your art, or you wearing the latest spring fashions with other people of note, or you at a party with other people of note. Sometimes the Man writes the reviews. In the theater, when I started, there was a critic, Frank Rich, who could shut your show down with the blink of an eye. He could also change your life for the better with what he wrote. That's what happened in my case: so I've felt the power of the Man and its effect in real ways.

The Man can be a man or a woman. The Man can be older than you or younger than you. The Man can be any color. More often they are white, but there are black men who are the Man; there are Asian men, some black women, some Latinos. The Man is anyone who is in power, anywhere in the world. George Bush is the Man. Osama bin Laden is the Man. Condoleezza Rice is the Man. Missy Elliott is the Man. Bruce Springsteen is the Man. The head of the Museum of Modern Art is the Man. P. Diddy Sean "Puffy" Combs is the Man. The Man is the one who can open the door, and the Man can shut you down.

The Man has the power.

But so do you. And my goal in writing to you is to make that clear.

Put this on your wall wherever you put things that mean something to you: *The Man has the power, but so do I.*

Listen, BZ: One day you might just be the Man.

ADS
Honolulu
April 2003

Exchanges

Dear BZ:

You were telling me about all the cliques in your school—the sports people, the rockers, the black kids, the Vietnamese kids, the granola kids, and so on and so on. I have been thinking about exchanges, and all the things we can learn from one another. I love meeting people with whom I have absolutely nothing in common. I have been having such an exchange with a man I just met: Michael Bentt. Michael was a world-champion boxer. He's been teaching me to box. But we do a lot more than box. We walk, we run, we skip rope. Most of all we talk while doing these things. Every single interaction is rich with new thoughts. He's teaching me to box, and I'm trying to share with him whatever I can about Shakespeare, because he's preparing to play Othello next fall.

I first saw Michael at a gym in West Hollywood, jumping rope. I could tell from the way that he jumped rope that he had been a professional boxer. I was intimidated by him because of this obvious athletic excellence. Talk about presence! Wow!

At the end of his workout, he came over and introduced himself, which surprised me. As it turns out he knew my work. "Ms. Smith," he said, "just wanted to say I'm a fan of your work." Turns out, he's an actor, too. He was in *Ali*, the film starring Will Smith as Muhammad Ali. He played Sonny Liston. He had won the world championship and had boxed on the U.S. boxing team. Now he wanted to talk to me about acting. I agreed to meet with him, but only if he would teach me to jump rope. We exchanged numbers, played phone tag, and when we finally connected he said, amused, "So, you want to learn to skip rope, huh?"

"I do," I said.

We met at a boxing gym in Hollywood. Small world—he knew a guy I had trained with in New York, a boxer named Eddie Cruz. And so my lessons started. I'm still at it. Since Michael had given me a couple of jump-rope lessons, it was my time to make good on the deal.

We met for coffee to talk about acting. We talked until we were kicked out of the place, then went down the street to another place and kept going. We could have talked all night, because the subject of freedom came up. And freedom is a complex topic.

Michael is a large black man who has the ability to knock a person out with his fists, yet he has a very soft voice. He told me that sometimes onstage, his voice just goes out—he tries to say his lines, and his voice just disappears. Michael was born in England to West Indian parents and raised in the United States. His father was very strict—and Michael was raised to keep his voice low, particularly because he is large.

But Michael was also trained as a boxer, and so he had a connection to his primal instincts, his survival instincts. As artists, we all need contact with our primal instincts—and for most of us these instincts are trained out of us, unless we are becoming warriors or fighters of any kind.

An artist needs fight. Michael is having trouble awakening that primal nature for acting, whereas it was readily available under the lights, in front of crowds, and in the boxing ring. "The thing you need for freedom," I told him, "is joy: the sheer joy of being there onstage—the joy, the adrenaline you feel when you are about to fight. The same thing applies to the stage."

I told him that when I was a kid, I was a fat kid, and it was absolute torture, for example, for me to walk onto a stage at a school assembly, because the entire school would collapse into fits of laughter the minute I walked out. Now why they did that is still a mystery to me. Our school was not so large. We knew one another by sight, so everyone had seen me before. Everyone knew I was fat. In fact, the year before at the very same assembly they would have seen that I was fat. Nonetheless, this was the ritual. I would walk out, they would laugh, and I would open my mouth to begin to speak. The moment I began to speak they would stop laughing.

Now, what gave me the courage to go out there every time? I was terrified the night before. I dreaded the laughter. I was too young to know or to trust that I would remember my lines—it was usually a poem, or something prepared. I once asked my mother why the teacher would give me (rather than another child) the poem to say, and she replied, "Because the teachers knew you would learn all your parts." And so it was. And so deep down inside, my passion, my desire to have my classmates hear "the parts" overrode the terror I had.

After I told him this, Michael shared with me that in fact he had stuttered in school, and the same thing had happened to him. (One of the best things about being an artist, BZ, is that solving problems always comes down to sharing vulnerabilities, sharing the things that make us human.) And so I talked to Michael about joy, about how every time he opens his mouth, he should experience a sense of joy that at this point in his life the stutter is gone, and that joy should fuel more volume in his voice. And we both set about talking about James Earl Jones, the great black actor who had stuttered as a child and who didn't speak for an extended period of time. Now, when we call information on a Verizon phone, it is the rich, low, full voice of James Earl Jones that we Americans hear.

I think that tapping into the sheer joy of whatever it is that you do—that is, when I go onstage, when you enter the studio to paint, when your cousin goes to ballet class—the sheer joy is what liberates us, opens the senses, the heart, the arteries, so that we feel that strong will to communicate that is greater than any chains we may have.

"Michael," I said, "the point is, we should be just plain glad that we can express things." I looked down at my watch. I was a half hour late for a dinner I was meant to be at. Clearly my passion for these ideas had overridden the chain of the clock.

Michael walked me to my car. "The reason I want to learn to jump rope," I said, coming to a sudden realization, "is that when I was a kid, a fat kid, I was horrible at it. I never was able to jump double Dutch or do any of the standard jump-rope things that the kids on my block did. So, silly as it sounds, I want to learn to jump rope to free my body of certain chains it put on long ago about jumping rope."

"Is that right?" he asked, slightly amused. He still didn't take my jump-rope practice seriously.

"And you," I said, crossing the street, heading to my car and calling back to him, "ought to take ballet lessons."

He grinned and said, "You know, maybe I will."

ADS
Beverly Hills
March 2003

Procrastination

Dear BZ:

So you say you're procrastinating. We all suffer from this from time to time.

We think of the procrastinator as lazy and inactive, but procrastination is *active*. Not to get all psychological and heavy on you, but procrastination is actually "active avoidance." I like the word *active*, because it shows just how powerful your avoidance tendencies are.

It takes all kinds of forms—writer's block and disorganization are two of the most common. I've known people who have mild forms of it, and I've known people who are absolutely crippled by it, who never accomplish what they have set out to do.

The more I work, the more I am impressed that a lot of people actually do work in a steady way that allows them to deliver on time and with full preparedness. If you are working with a group of people, you really do hang things up if you procrastinate. The most heavy-handed thing I can say is: If you procrastinate, you are only robbing yourself.

I am in awe of the power of procrastination. I am so in awe of it that if I have something I have to do, I try to program myself to do it so quickly that procrastination cannot possibly set in. At one point I was so afraid of not fulfilling my commitment to swim every day that I slept in my bathing suit! I would sleep in my suit, throw on a swim parka at five A.M., and, without thinking about it, head to my car and off to the pool.

The main fuel for procrastination is thought. Sometimes procrastination abounds because you really don't have a clear idea of what you are trying to do, and where it's going. Then the exercise of visualizing what you are trying to do, what you want, what your goal is, can be helpful.

If you are basically a motivated person, without too many deep, dark reasons why you are conflicted about success, then procrastination can be met head-on by "just doing it." Give yourself an image of what you are trying to do, and just start. The doing gives you energy and ideas. If I swim a mile, the first half hour might be drudgery, but somewhere in the middle it catches fire.

Some great writer, when asked if he liked to write, said: "I like to have written." We all like to be finished, so we can look back. There's no way out of procrastination, or *active* avoidance, but to move.

Some people say they work best under pressure, but working under pressure is a bit of a fallacy. It's not waiting till the last minute that gives you the good work; it's the focus that is required when you wait till the last minute that brings about the good work. So think of it this way: Your focus is the center of your brilliance; why not avail yourself of that brilliance on a regular basis? Everyone has her own rhythm, but if you don't like the fact that you procrastinate, one way to get out of it is to think of what the alternative is. The alternative is, instead of trying to do a month's work in a few intense days in the studio, to give yourself the pleasure of yourself *in flow*, *in focus*, on a regular basis.

ADS

Trust

Dear BZ:

You are a post–9/11 person. By that I mean the greater part of your life will have been lived after September 11, 2001.

We are all living in an unsteady time. We are at war. America appears to be going into a dramatically different period in its history. We are not sure what the future holds. It is hard for many of us to feel that we have an impact on the course of the country and the course of the world. When your grandchildren read about our time in history books, they will see that artists were a part of it, but while we are in the moment, it's hard to see who has impact other than warriors, politicians, the media, and businessmen/women.

During the 1996 presidential campaign, I traveled with various candidates, and with Jesse Jackson. Jackson is a very charismatic speaker. He would end every speech with a chant—"Keep . . . hope . . . alive! Keep . . . hope . . . alive!"

I think that in this day and age, the chant should be "Keep trust alive."

This will be harder for us than we think.

There are so many obstacles to creating solid trusts. We trust only those whom we can rely on.

In order to keep trust alive, we must start with ourselves. We start with making ourselves trustworthy. Which is an easy thing to do. Real substantial trust will come from real substantial doings. It can be as simple as being on time, being honest, being discreet, doing the work you say you'll do, keeping promises, being loyal. It can be as simple as being prepared, going the extra mile, giving someone the benefit of the doubt when no one else will, choosing commitment to an idea, a principle, or a belief over popularity. It is bred by being there for someone when things are not going well. To become trustworthy is no small thing. It requires self-knowledge. It requires clarity about your own principles. It requires being a grown-up. Being a grown-up has nothing to do with age. I have met people at sixteen who are grown-ups. I have met people who are sixty who are not.

Once you are trustworthy, it might follow that you will also bring into the circle around yourself and your work others who are trustworthy in the same way. This is how trust is kept alive: by you, first of all, being trustworthy.

Charlayne Hunter-Gault is a journalist who, in the early days of the U.S. civil rights movement, was the first black woman to go to the University of Georgia. When I interviewed her, she said, "I always watch my back; I don't trust anybody. I trust myself."

I believe it's important to be able to trust others—but ultimately you should never find yourself in a position where you trust someone else more than you trust yourself.

ADS

The Pen Is Mightier Than the Sword

Dear BZ:

There are certain basics that you need.

In the old days (by that I mean in my mother's generation) they'd say a woman needed one suit, a pair of gloves, and a hat, and a man needed a navy-blue suit and a brown suit. Closets are a lot more complicated these days, and in another way a lot simpler. You could probably get away with jeans almost anywhere, if you had the correct accessories and the correct shoes.

But I would like to go further than clothing as a metaphor when I talk about the basic kit for an artist. I'd like to think of the artist's situation in terms of *real* survival, not just social survival.

I want to talk about not just what you look like when you enter a room, but more about how you engage and interact in that room. Not just what kind of impression you make, but what you actually do and cause to change by your presence. Not just the rules you have to follow, but how you change the rules. Not just what you take from a given situation, but what you leave and what you give. I want to look at not just what you leave behind, but how you manage to push people forward before you leave.

For that I am going to look to war for a metaphor. Elizabeth Neuffer was a friend of mine. She was a war correspondent for the *Boston Globe*. When she was preparing to go to Afghanistan in 2001, I talked to her while she was packing. She needed batteries for her cell phone, some dried fruits and nuts, which were easy to carry, proper clothes, and so forth. Those would have been expected. What surprised me was that the last thing she did before leaving was to go to Bloomingdale's department store in New York City, where she got samples of perfume. Not for herself. These were gifts that would not take up a lot of space in her suitcase, and she could carry a lot of them. She would give them out after interviews as a way of saying thanks. And you know what else she packed? Pens. She would also be giving out pens, saying as she did so to children in Afghanistan, as she had done in Bosnia and Rwanda: "The pen is mightier than the sword. Use this one."

It's tough to take your art into the world, really into the world. I don't mean, necessarily, in a way that makes you famous, but in a way that makes your art relevant to the world. The way Elizabeth made her writing. When she died, there was a wonderful photo of her displayed at the memorial service, where she was down on her knee, with her pen and reporter's notebook, just resting, while she listened intently to a weeping woman—her presence offering, I am sure, consolation. As you develop, look for communities of people, some who are artists and some who are not, who believe that art can make a difference. Find partners in other disciplines.

I hope that the lessons I learned the hard way are things that you can assume to know as givens. 1) You can't waste time trying to get approval from the people who you assume hold your fate in their hands. 2) You should be a part of making a new fate—not just for you, not just for other artists, but for others. 3) As artists, we make culture. We should take that seriously. The animals know how to survive through DNA. Humans know how to survive through watching and studying culture. You are the generation that could make a difference. 4) My generation got stuck on itself. Unstick us.

ADS
San Francisco
April 2004

For Rent

Dear BZ:

As an actress I feel that my identity is for rent. Not for sale. But for rent.

ADS
Hollywood, California
February 2002

relationships

Struggling Artists

Dear BZ:

Some people love spring, others summer. I don't know that many people who say they love winter—although I love snow blizzards in New York City because they're beautiful and because they shut the city down, make it quiet, and bring special images like people cross-country skiing down the historic streets of SoHo or Tribeca. And I love winter by the ocean on Long Island. And in Idaho. It's refreshing.

I especially like fall—because it's full of promise. I like the feeling of the air when it just starts getting cold, like at the end of September, and you have to go from a sweater to a jacket, or a sweater under a light jacket. You are still free to walk without the bulk of winter clothing, and yet there is something quite wonderful about the feel of the extra wool, or cotton, or whatever fiber you choose to warm you up.

The first time I moved to New York, in 1976, it was summer—a long, hot, humid, imprisoning summer. I had been living in San Francisco, where I had gone to graduate school. At that time, everything about New York was challenging. I wore white socks and Birkenstock sandals, a mainstay in San Francisco. In New York they were not practical. I'd come home at the end of the day and my socks would be completely covered with soot and dirt. Birkenstocks and white socks looked too much like hippie culture—too "granola," as the saying used to go, for the concrete and the fast pace of New

York. People now look on New York in those days and assert that it was a "wild" place.

By the next year I knew a lot more about how to "be." And most important, I had found a friend. A true friend, as distinguished from even a lover. This was a friend who I knew would be a friend for life. And that is a special, special feeling, a special, special find. A soul mate.

On the surface, we weren't much alike. Randy was a handsome white guy from Flint, Michigan. He had blue eyes and light brown hair that he wore cropped close to his head. He had no college education, but he was highly educated from the way he had lived his life already. He was twenty-one or twenty-two; he lived at the Y in a small room, with space for little more than his sleeping bag. He had removed his bed from his room in order to have space for things he was collecting: cameras, rugs he'd gotten while traveling. He slept on the floor.

We met in a restaurant where we both worked. It was a soul-food restaurant in the Village on the corner of Charles and Bleecker, right in the heart of the West Village. The people who ran it were not particularly nice, and the work was very hard. One of them had done something called "est," which had, in my opinion, a kind of repressive orthodoxy—about how to live your life, how to get ahead, etc.—a kind of a "mind" movement. Everyone who worked close to him had this orthodoxy. This made everything have a certain weight. It felt . . . well, fascistic.

The place was large. It was owned, or had been owned, by two gay men, one black and one white. We rarely saw them. They had a very tight management staff. The waitstaff was composed of waiters, bartenders, bus people, assistant managers, and managers. You had to do time as a bus person for several months before becoming a waiter. The prime jobs were hostesses and bartenders, because they automatically got a cut of the tips. It was not clear how one could rise to those positions.

The restaurant was known for its corn bread. The bus people were lowest on the totem pole. At the end of the long evening, before we were allowed to leave, the managers would come around with a flashlight and make sure that there were no corn bread crumbs on the floor of our areas of the room. These managers, by the way, were our peers. Most of us, professionally, were in the same boat.

Almost everyone who worked at this place was an aspiring artist of some kind or another—dancers, singers, visual artists, a few models. Everyone was from a different background—some were educated; others had come to New York from points far and wide with no training, just a "dream." Most of us were working in order to make enough money to take classes, or get photographs made and reproduced for our portfolios, etc. And, of course, to pay the rent. It was a kind of back-and-forth. You'd work enough to make enough money to take a class. You'd take the class, be broke, stop and wait to make more money. We were all waiting tables so we could be free to audition or otherwise market our wares during the day.

Every day, when we arrived at work, a large "congress" of waiters and bus people would come to a meeting, over which one of the owners' right-hand people presided. There were different ones, but the one I remember best was a short, very well built, openly gay man with cropped blond hair, who was impeccably neat. He looked like one of Hitler's youth. The rest of us were given the tasks of either folding napkins, checking saltshakers, putting fresh butter into ramekins and smoothing it out, or snapping green beans. Green beans are a mainstay of soul food, when cooked with some form of pork.

I was kind of excited about having the job because I'd never had a job as a waitress. I thought I had to pretend I was not very smart, because obedience seemed to be very important. (I associated obedience with intellectual poverty.) It was also important not to ask too many questions, because even a fair question could be mistaken for a challenge or an assertion of will. There was one black man there, and I don't recall there being any other black women who worked there. The black man was a very good-looking person, who was a dancer. For the first week or so I kept my mouth shut and tried my best to do my job—which consisted of removing plates, putting down corn bread and water, emptying ashtrays (people smoked in restaurants in those days), and carrying large plastic buckets of dirty dishes to the kitchen and trying to do so without slipping on lettuce and all the other kinds of food that landed on the floor and got mixed with water and grime.

One day I looked up from snapping green beans, and Randy was sitting across from me, snapping green beans. He was the first person in this "est" atmosphere who had the slightest hint of irony on his face. He seemed to be looking straight at me, and he was. He saw that underneath my veil of obedience was an idea that everything we were doing was ridiculous. I was surprised to see his glance, but it did not waver, and I smiled back. I was surprised that this muscular blond with startling blue eyes found a kinship with me in those few seconds while snapping green beans. And I felt a kinship with him. That's how a close friendship of almost thirty years began. Over green beans, napkins, and butter ramekins.

I managed to do that job without getting fired. The highlight of it all was pouring water for James Baldwin, who said when I was just moving out of earshot, "She reminds me of Lorraine." I took it he meant Lorraine Hansberry—and I assumed he was referring to me. (Who knew if he was? But the fantasy kept me going.) Lorraine Hansberry had always been a symbol of intellectual freedom. To hear her name evoked just as I had placed corn bread in front of James Baldwin, another icon, was—Wow! To me the restaurant had been like a plantation, and any little hint that there might be a way out was exciting.

By the end of the summer, Randy and I both moved "uptown," so to speak. I got a job teaching acting to children in Harlem. He had gotten a job at a very fancy French restaurant on the Upper East Side, frequented by Jackie O and other celebrities. He was at the restaurant for a few years. He learned about fine foods, wines, design and fashion, and good manners just by being there, and he taught me everything he learned. He then moved to another fancy French restaurant downtown, where he still works. The key is this—he works only part of the year; the rest of the time he is traveling around the world taking photographs. I went from the job in Harlem to teaching at Carnegie Mellon to USC to Stanford to NYU. I do that only part of the year; the rest of the year I am traveling to work or to learn about people in other places and with other lifestyles. Same as Randy.

That fall was full of newness. The air seemed to hold magic as Randy and I would explore a museum, learn about a new champagne, or find yet another reason that we had a spiritual kinship. We traveled together. We went to see where John Brown was hanged in Virginia. We leafed through fashion magazines. He introduced me to his singing teacher, who had ancient recordings of opera singers and who had buckets and buckets of stories and gossip. We talked and talked.

There's nothing like those years when you don't yet have what you are working for. There's a lot of freedom because there's so much possibility. You need friends who are working for something, too. I just reread "Sweet Lorraine," an essay that James Baldwin wrote about Lorraine Hansberry. They talked, and argued, and tried to figure things out. There were so many nights such as those that I spent with Randy. You don't have to be Lorraine Hansberry or James Baldwin to have those nights. You just need some dreams and something to fret about and someone to dream and fret with. America, as a nation, I am told, wrote and talked itself into existence. Everything starts with an all-night conversation. Find a spiritual twin to walk the city streets with, to waken the dawn with, to construct a world with.

ADS
New York City
October 2003

Agents, Gallery Owners, Managers, Lawyers, Publicists, Accountants, Bookkeepers, and So Forth

Dear BZ:

Artists are vulnerable to complicating the high that accompanies success, and to getting drowned by the profound disappointment that accompanies failure (or, better said, expectations that are not met). We can confuse those highs and lows with a general estimation of personal value—that is, by making a judgment about our value as human beings.

This is true in all professions and human interactions to some degree, but I believe that artists are particularly vulnerable. Both "success" and "failure" are usually, in the arts, judged in relation to expectations, and often cannot really be "calculated" in advance. Louis Pasteur, the brilliant scientist who developed pasteurization, told us, "Chance favors the prepared mind."

How do you prepare for something that is, in part, based on chance? The only answer is, prepare anyway. Just in case. I'll use the profession of acting as an example. Yet look at potentially how *little* agency an actor has. Before a television show goes on the air and becomes a part of American culture, before an actor becomes a household name, there is a long process that leads to one significant stage—the stage of becoming a "pilot." When the show is selected to be a pilot, plans are made to produce it as one episode, which is then tried before some audiences and, of course, many executives. On that basis a decision is made whether to put it on the air. It may then go on the air, but all along the way it can be taken off the air if it does not get good ratings. It might stay on the air for many years, or it might not. The first major measure of a show's success is whether it can last for three years. This is very difficult, and there are many, many, many things that can happen in the first three years that do not allow the show to stand the test of time.

What amazes me is that at all levels of conversation—with agents, with producers, with writers, with directors, with executives at studios and television networks—it is almost impossible to have a discussion about why something works or does not work that goes beyond a mere shoulder shrug, and an utterance of "We'll just have to see" or "We got lucky." In no other profession would this be the case.

If you are an actor, before you go to an audition for a television pilot, or have a meeting, or agree to do one, you must sign a contract. The contract binds you to the project for six years, with, on the other hand, no guarantee that you'll have work for six years. *In other words, the actors are obligated to the producers, and have to make a commitment to them, but the producers have no real obligations to the actors.* Always find out how things work. You must balance that with your desire to focus on your art and keep it "pure."

You also have to be armed with knowing all acceptable procedures. It is not enough to get the job. You have to know everything you can about how the systems work and what is fair to expect and not fair to expect. The more successful you are, the more layers of protection of your interest surround you. Until that time, you must be armed with information, common sense, and presence of mind.

Put this on your wall—mental or imagined: *It is not enough to get the job. You must personally, intimately know, for yourself, the workings of the system around the job.*

You should understand what is expected of you. You may not get everything you want in a contract—but you must be fully conscious of what you are getting, what you are not getting, and what you are expected to deliver. And you cannot be in a blur or have other anxieties when you read these agreements.

Many people who would like to be in business with you will approach you as if they are your best friend. It's a very personable sort of field. People will appear to be "protecting" you. In my art form, we actors seem to be the most vulnerable, in part because of our training and psychological makeup. If you have ever watched a group of actors leaving rehearsal, for example, they generally kiss and hug good-bye. I've never seen a group of stockbrokers doing that, or doctors, or lawyers. In the arts we tend to be . . . well . . . more touchy. Is it that way in the world of painting? In acting, dance, and music, words like *darling*, *sweetheart*, *sugar* abound. Not so much for men as for women. Regardless of the displays of warmth and affection, it is still a business.

The most important thing to understand is this: From the moment you sell a work, or desire to sell a work, you are in *business*. The world around artists sometimes infantilizes them. I think this is in part because our educational systems decide at some point that art is infantile (and from what you tell me, this seems to be the case at your school). In the United States, for the most part, we stop encouraging children to imagine by third grade. So it seems that the endeavors of an artist, no matter how *un*childlike they are, are "childish." To be in business, you have to be an adult.

I teach at the School of the Arts, and I work also at the law school at NYU. I am not saying my graduate students in performance are any less mature than the law students. Yet artists are often expected to put their insights on hold, while waiting to adhere to the whims of those people who own the space in which art is made and displayed. That's a *fact*.

How do you put those two things together? How do you manage to have grace in the face of authority and not alienate those in power, and at the same time keep your integrity and make a contribution? First of all, understand that even authority figures will gain from interacting with you. The figure of authority is not static. You may actually be able to help figures of authority imagine another way of doing things. Not just through your art, but by *how* you are in business.

Integrate your imagination into your life. This will have more meaning when you are in the business of art, but I think it is something you can practice now with the principal of your school, your teachers, and others who seem to have authority *over* you. Ask yourself, "Who are they?" "What matters to them?" "How can I speak to what their priorities are?" "How can that be a strategy for getting them to change a policy?" "Is there any business to what we are involved in here?" (There is business involved in public education, by the way: business and politics.) "When they talk to me, can I hear what they are saying, or am I a blur either because I am invested in pleasing them, or because I am invested in displeasing them?" "Am I afraid of their authority?" "Why?"

If you never come in contact with authority figures—

either because they frighten you or because you find them irrelevant—question that immediately. Do not hide from them. Do not discount them. Learn how to have a relationship with authority.

Will you be a person who strives to please authority: to paint paintings that comfort them? Or will you be a provocateur? Or something in between? The relationships of artists to governments, regimes, patrons, producers have been explored by artists over the centuries. Examine these relationships. Look at the work of an artist, not just in terms of whether it is aesthetically interesting to you. Find out—what was this artist's relationship to his/her society at the time, to his/her banker, to his/her lovers, to his/her family? Rehearse this now—you will need these muscles as much as you need the ability to draw.

I talked about these issues recently with a friend who works with a very powerful, very influential talent agency. She had formerly worked in the Clinton White House for many years and on a variety of political campaigns. I consider her to be "savvy." She said to me, "You are in a dumb business. I am in a smart business. Acting is a dumb business. Agenting is a smart business."

Which is true. Artists are in a business in which there is absolutely no direct relationship between effort and success. An agent draws a commission on your success. A lawyer is paid to help you protect your success, and your intellectual property, etc. All of these people provide a service. To a greater or lesser extent they are a part of helping create your career.

Then I spoke with someone who had worked in both Bush administrations. She is now a major executive in a big communications conglomerate. The conversation went like this:

I said, "(So and so) told me—'You are in a dumb business. I am in a smart business. Acting is a dumb business. Agenting is a smart business.'"

She replied, "That's exactly right. You're looking for gold and she's selling shovels."

But let's look at these ideas for a minute. There's another way to see this. I am on the board of the Museum of Modern Art. What I see on the faces of the board members is the thrill at the prospect of finding gold. In this case the gold is, in fact, the *art* and the *artists*. I went on a studio visit and watched some members of the board listen to the exciting painter/printmaker Ellen Gallagher discuss her work. They were enchanted. We artists are not the only ones seeking the gold. There are others looking for gold: the gold being that which is engaging and enchanting, that which relates to the past, present, and future.

Yet for all the leadership artists provide by leading people to see *their lives* in a broader context, they still find themselves in the position of a child in their relationships with people who are there to help create the business of their careers. To increase your sales and your presence in the world you need partners. Your presence is normally connected to sales—either sales of your product or sales of your ideas. You may be worried about the health of your idea or the health of the mechanism you use to communicate your idea. Your friends who dance are trying to create a kind of body through exercise and diet and rehearsal. Your friends who sing are trying to develop their voices. But along with these personal developments, a kind of external development has to happen. In schools, few curricula for the artist combine these two kinds of learning in a balanced and cohesive way.

Being an artist is very hard work. Not only do you have to constantly develop your discipline, but if you have a desire to make a living, you have to be a good businessperson.

Agents, business managers, etc., etc., are not the authors of your career. They make suggestions. They are a part of your research team. You are the author. You are the center of your career. You have to run the show. I hope your show is about more than gold digging. I hope your show is about becoming the most engaging, enchanting, magical person that you can be—*through* your art. Art is ultimately transcendent. That's a fact.

ADS
Le Montrose Suite Hotel
West Hollywood, California
February 2004

Dealing with the Man (or Your Power)

Dear BZ:

In ancient times, the poets had patrons—or "friends." The poets were poor; the patrons were rich. Our economic system does not really require that we have "patrons" in the same way they did in antiquity. Artists do have sponsors, donors, and funders, and often organizations have patrons or donors. So to some extent we do still have them today. Sometimes we are reenacting an ancient, and perhaps classic, perhaps natural relationship. A patron is often different from the Man. Sometimes patrons employ someone who is the Man to work with you more directly. Sometimes the patrons, as much as they may enjoy your work, need the Man in order to keep you in line.

Although the Man is not the same as a boss, he or she can have other kinds of authority over you. The Man, after all, is trying to make money with your talent. Sometimes the Man will misuse his or her power, in all of the same ways that powerful people in other businesses and professions misuse power.

Here are some concrete dos and don'ts. When you go to meet with the Man, have a list. You can either memorize it or have it in front of you. Never go to a meeting with the Man without that list, or "script." Know exactly what you are going to say to the Man and what you are going to ask him/her for. Don't improvise. Keep the list short.

When preparing a list for the Man, don't think for the Man. Don't think, "Oh, he/she will think this is ridiculous"—just go for it.

It's better if you can tell the Man what *he* or *she* needs, rather than verbalizing it in a way that seems to be about what *you* need. Let the Man see what you can give, not just what you would like him or her to give. All day long people are coming to the Man, saying what they need or what they don't have. The Man will be relieved to find someone in his/her presence who *seems to be thinking about the Man.*

Sometimes meetings with the Man are socially uncomfortable. It can be hard to get a grip on the meeting. For example, what do you do when you have a very talkative "Man"? The proportion of talk could go like this: The Man talks for half an hour or even forty-five minutes about things in general—usually things that he/she has had to fight for, usually stories of victory—and you talk for ten minutes. At the end of the fifty-five minutes, where the Man has spoken for forty-five minutes and I have spoken for ten, I am never completely sure that he has heard me. If you have a meeting with someone like that, you have to be piercingly prepared, so that what you say is really resonant. And you have to be extremely clear about what you want and what you have to give the Man.

On the other hand, you could get a nonverbal "Man," who doesn't talk. The meeting might start, "What can I do for you?" I suppose the worst start of a meeting would be one in which a nonspeaking, nonsmiling "Man" simply glances at his/her watch.

You can rehearse these meetings with friends and offer to rehearse their meetings with you.

To make this practical, let's talk about you in your life right now. In your school, BZ, you have almost no arts program. In your school, who is the Man? Is it the principal? Is it the superintendent? Is it the mayor? Is it the PTA? Get with a group of your friends and make it a point to discover who the Man is. Begin to prepare now, to see who you need to talk to and how you need to talk to them to turn this around. Anything is possible. It starts with you and a group of people who talk often. Your conversations need to be about what you would *like* to see, not about what you see already.

I want to accomplish several things in these letters, among them:

1) to let you know that the Man exists, and that you *always* have to deal with the Man. The Man is important to your survival;

2) to give you some strategies for dealing with the Man.

You have something the Man needs. You have your art, which the Man will promote so that he/she will make money or get cultural power by being associated with your art.

The most important thing to keep in mind while dealing with the Man is that he/she is, in fact, after all, just a man.

ADS

Support

Hi, BZ:

An artist needs support—not just money, but support. And more often than not, truly progressive people do not get the support they need.

I'm thinking about this because I've just given a speech to a group of philanthropists—they give away money. It's more political than you would imagine. A group of us went for drinks after my presentation. They were all funders—from various kinds of foundations. Most of them were liberal in their outlook, politically and socially—I'd go so far as to say that some are progressive. We talked about how liberal funding organizations are much less likely to fund "infrastructure." By this I mean the stuff that supports an artist on a regular basis and keeps things going—just like, in a town, you have to have highways, garbage collection, bookkeeping, etc. Liberal funders often want to see grassroots work, but they don't want to fund organizational structure or support.

Here's something you can do about it right now. Don't be an art snob! You may be hanging only with artists. That's a mistake. Make friends in all areas. Make friends with people who are headed to business school. Broaden your arena to people in your school who are going to be lawyers, who want to have businesses—who are entrepreneurial, who like to organize things. You need to know a lot about different kinds of people and how they think—What matters to them? What are their personalities? What kinds of books and magazines do they read? What Web sites do they visit? You will be a kind of an entrepreneur yourself. Besides, you should develop relationships now that you plan to use for the rest of your life and career. It's always good to have people from your past whom you can trust—even for different kinds of advice. Build a brain trust for yourself.

And who knows, you may be able to make a difference someday. If you've got a friend from high school who ends up in a foundation where no one trusts artists, you might be able to swing him/her another way. What if you have a friend who is headed to run a corporation? Maybe your influence could cause that CEO to buy art for the buildings or to sit on the board of an arts institution. Maybe you should befriend someone who's going to become a cop. Your influence might help him/her look beyond stereotypes. And it works both ways. Your friends can broaden your scope, too.

ADS
Toronto, Canada
April 2004

Jealousy

Dear BZ:

Jealousy? Hmmm. Jealousy links up with competition. It's hard to compete, really compete, in the art world. That's why award ceremonies are a little suspect. Athletes can compete; businesses can compete. I don't know how much you can really compete as an artist. You can compete with yourself.

You are an explorer. You understand that every time you go into the studio, you are after something that *does not yet exist.* Maybe it's the same for a runner. I don't know. But with running, or swimming, or gymnastics, or tennis, the achievement is measurable. Forget about competition. Rather, commit yourself to find out the true nature of your art. How does it really work; what's the essence of it? Go for that thing that no one can teach you. Go for that communion, that real communion with your soul, and the discipline of expressing that communion to others. That doesn't come from competition. That comes from being one with what you are doing. It comes from concentration, and from your own ability to be fascinated endlessly with the story, the song, the jump, the color you are working with.

I know this sounds a little monkish or even sort of "holier than thou," but I really do believe it. And that said, jealousy *is* a human sentiment. Few of us are above it. John Lahr, a writer, told me that the major emotion in Los Angeles is envy. I have to say he's probably right. And a lot of it has to do with how close to or far from an Academy Award one is. And LA, the capital of smoke and mirrors, would have some believe that the award is just a step away. When you drive down Hollywood Boulevard, some of those dreamers look as though the dream ate them alive.

Keep it real. Even jealousy is based on fantasies: a fantasy that someone else has what belongs to you.

ADS
Los Angeles

Mentors

Dear BZ:

Your question "How did you find your mentors?" is a good one. I sought them out on my own, and they came from all sorts of backgrounds. Many of them were unexpected. They are not all actors, or writers, or artists, for that matter. Tonight I had dinner with someone I consider a mentor: Studs Terkel. More on that in a moment.

My dentist is a mentor. She is a fascinating woman who survived the Holocaust. She taught herself physics and chemistry in order to get into medical school. Out of a time of extraordinary hardship, she came to this country with a man who became an executive at Chanel. She is probably the only dentist who wears Chanel shoes along with her white coat. She is one of the most down-to-earth people I know, with an ability to focus with razor-sharp intensity. I tell her I love her clothes and her accent. She sounds like a Viennese psychiatrist. She was born in Poland, and was educated in England. I was sent to her in New York because I'd just gone to a dentist who, in the middle of a procedure, had said, "Whoops!" Imagine my anxiety when I landed in her chair for the first time. It was her job to repair what the other dentist had done. I can't tell you what she exudes. It's not false confidence. I trusted her immediately. The ability to engender trust, as we've discussed before, is a huge asset in this day and age. So she's my mentor for that.

As I said, she survived the Holocaust. She was a very young girl in Poland and had been hidden in a convent. She was hidden in a small room by herself, with no toys, nothing. They were afraid she would talk and give herself away if the Gestapo came, because she was too little to know the difference. I did not know about her past until I had been her patient for over ten years. When I learned her story, I thought about a gesture that she had. Just before giving an injection, she would say, "This will hurt a little bit" (unlike many dentists, who say, "It won't hurt," or who say nothing at all, unless you ask). After saying, "This will hurt a little," she gives the injection and then she puts her hand to your cheek and holds it tightly. She knows something about pain.

Mentors are different from teachers in general because you pick them. You seek them out, or sometimes they declare themselves as your mentor. I suppose in the strict sense of the word, a mentor is someone who takes the responsibility of "schooling you," showing you the ropes, bringing you through the system. I think of them also as inspirational people who have broken ground or lit a path.

And now Studs. I consider Studs Terkel, the great radio man, a mentor. Studs did interviews on the radio for years. He has written several books. I don't know very many people who are as truly learned as he is. I always marvel that he knows so much. He is now ninety years old. He has a hard time hearing. Tonight, at dinner, I had to yell to be heard. He knows a lot about America politically and culturally, and has interviewed thousands of people, from regular working people to Martin Luther King. One of his best friends was the great gospel singer Mahalia Jackson. When I visit him in Chicago, all kinds of people approach him, but it never feels as though he is a "celebrity" in that sense—more that he's a man about town, a part of the community whom many people have an attachment to, or an association with. Just the fact that he's out there puts me on a path and lights the way.

Although it's important to make communities with like-minded people—people who are your age, your generation, who are working on projects that have resonance with yours—I am a firm believer in crossing generations to find mentorship and inspiration, and a sense of furthering the craft. So I'd say that as you begin to seek mentorship, be creative about where you look. Look in unlikely places. It will enrich your work. It will broaden your work, and make it more likely that you will cross boundaries and reach a wider, more culturally and intellectually diverse audience.

ADS
Chicago
February 2002

Reaching Out

Dear BZ:

As you know, I've been teaching at New York University. On Saturday my teaching assistant was trying to locate a student. She called a referral number on his cell phone and ended up speaking to the student's mother, who was crying. A friend of her son's, a student, had committed suicide by jumping off of the balcony into the atrium of the university library. I immediately called the mother myself and found out that this was the third suicide since the summer at NYU. I had not known about the previous deaths.

That Monday I met with my students and asked them about what had happened. They all seemed frightened and confused. Several of the graduate students wept. One male student sobbed and sobbed and sobbed.

When I talked to them they talked about alienation.

"But why do you feel alienated?" I said, feeling like I was totally out of their reality. "You're smart, you're attractive, you're at this school that's hard to get into, you can afford to be here, or have figured out how to get the money to be here. I am in New York because I *don't* feel alienated here, so this is puzzling. There is so much life here to observe. There are so many different standards of behavior and ideas about what is appropriate and not appropriate. I think I'd feel alienated in Kansas."

In the end I suggested that they try to suspend their personal feeling of alienation, and look instead for alienation in others and offer consolation when they see it. I gave them an exercise to prepare for the next class. They were to go around New York and find the loneliest person in the world. They were to observe that person, and then come in and reenact five minutes of what they saw. They had to reenact what they saw that person doing and how he or she was. They then had to find someone who was in the midst of offering a helping hand and reenact that.

Artists, as students of the human condition in all its dimensions—from joy and ecstasy to the depths of despair—don't necessarily have to experience that range of emotion themselves in real life. In other words, we can be happy artists—but we must learn to communicate those other feelings as if they were ours. Many artists have indeed suffered, and felt alienated, to the point of taking their own lives. But this is not a requirement for making art, obviously. What *is* required for making art is insatiable curiosity.

A healthy artist may have all of those feelings, but finds a way to be, as we have discussed, "both inside and outside" of a situation at the same time. An artist finds a way to be both participant and observer. This calls for an open heart and mind, and the ability to watch, observe, and absorb. And, as I have discussed, it is very important that you take care of yourself physically and emotionally. A dancer playing the Hunchback of Notre Dame needs a very flexible spine. Same is true of the actor playing Richard III.

So even as you may find yourself in a period of alienation, one strategy is to look for it in others. It may both relieve your own feeling and help you understand your feeling. Developing as an artist is a process of reaching out *from*. That is different from avoidance and denial; it is reaching out *from* your pain, to see and understand the pain of others.

We are doctors of sorts, doctors of the soul.

ADS
New York City
October 2003

Find Your Twin

Dear BZ:

I am in Lima, Peru. I'm exhausted after many hours of rehearsal, but exhilarated. I just saw, last night, the most dazzling performance. It is the work of a performance artist from São Paulo, Brazil, called Denise Stoklos. I can't describe it. It's not dance, it's not mime, it's not theater; it's something else. She calls it "the Essential Theater."

In her book she writes, "I want the stage naked. Rhythm and space themselves already bring theater diagrams plenty of riches."

She is a wild-looking person, and I don't think she would mind my saying that. She has wild blond hair with long dark roots. I was very taken with her performance, as you can tell. It turns out she was taken with a performance of mine she saw in New York.

And so we met for half an hour, huddled over a coffee in the café here at the Student Center, at a university in Lima.

We were born the same year. It is amazing how much we have in common. I feel I have met a twin. A spiritual twin. Years ago, I said I would travel the world to find one, and I have.

I promised to come to Brazil to see her before the year is out. "Really?" she said, in her deep voice and Brazilian accent. "Really." And I will.

These are the exchanges through art that make the world seem manageable.

Start looking for your twin in unlikely places. And don't forget it's especially exciting if you find your twin someplace that you could barely imagine yourself being. Go far away from what is familiar to you to find your twin.

ADS
Lima, Peru
July 2002

work

The West Wing

Dear BZ:

I just got a call from my agent saying that there's a job for me on a television show called *The West Wing*. Have you seen it? It's written by Aaron Sorkin, who wrote a movie called *The American President,* which I am in. And the actor Martin Sheen, whom I adore (and who was also in *The American President*), is in it.

I don't think I'm going to do the show. I am sort of swamped here, and can't imagine being able to get away to do it. I'm running the Institute on the Arts and Civic Dialogue. The president of the Ford Foundation is coming to visit, and you have no idea how much we have to do to prepare for her visit.

Anyway, what have you heard about this show? Have you watched it? What do you think of it?

ADS
Harvard University
Cambridge, Massachusetts
July 2000

The West Wing II

Dear BZ:

You're funny! You think I'd be a fool not to do *The West Wing*?

I take it you're a fan. It's just that I'm a producer up here at Harvard, the responsibility is mine, so I think I'd better sit tight.

In the meantime, send me your synopsis of the show and tell me about the characters.

The role they have in mind for me is National Security Advisor. You should see the lines I would have to say. Greek to me! Weapons. Planes. What's a "Night Hawk"?

ADS
Harvard University
Cambridge, Massachusetts
July 2000

The West Wing III

Dear BZ:

My publicist agrees with you—he's saying, "Get on that plane, and go to LA!!!" He says *The West Wing* is a big hit.

Well, off I go. I've got a copy of the script. It'll be phenomenal if I can speak this language.

Interesting that they are casting a black woman as National Security Advisor. I read in the *New York Times* that my Stanford colleague Condoleezza Rice may become National Security Advisor if George Bush becomes president. I wonder if that's what Aaron is thinking about?

ADS
Harvard University
Cambridge, Massachusetts
July 2000

The West Wing IV

Dear BZ:

Really interesting thing happened. I got to the set, and I saw Aaron Sorkin. I asked him if he cast me as the National Security Advisor because he's expecting that, in reality, Condoleezza Rice will become National Security Advisor. He said, "Who?" I guess that makes me the first black woman National Security Advisor.

ADS
Le Montrose Suite Hotel
West Hollywood, California
July 2000

The West Wing V

Dear BZ:

I'm waiting to take the red-eye back to Cambridge. I finished at *The West Wing* about three hours ago, and have some downtime here.

What a great show! The language is so rich—very unusual for television, or film for that matter. The actors, the director, the guy who does my makeup, are all terrific. The makeup artist was talking to me about his favorite magazine: *The Economist*.

It's always hard to say good-bye when you work for only a few days. I have a longing for the culture of working one job day in and day out, which is what most of this cast does.

Thanks for leading me in the right direction to take the job. Other than the fact that the names of the weapons are almost impossible to get out of your mouth without your tongue getting tripped up, it's—as they say—a great gig. Gosh, how humiliating to have them call out "cut" because I can't get my tongue around "Night Hawks" and planes going over places like Pyongyang Bay. And with Martin Sheen and John Spencer waiting patiently for me to get it right! And the actors were *so* nice. They all said about the language, "Welcome to *The West Wing*. The words are hard for all of us."

ADS
Los Angeles Airport
July 2000

Auditioning, Selling Your Wares

Dear BZ:

I'm writing you this on my BlackBerry in Van Nuys, California. Sitting in my car. It's hot out here. I just went inside to audition for a movie that Queen Latifah is making. The auditions are quite a trek from LA. In traffic. When I arrived, there was one other actress there. We were both early. The casting directors were walking back and forth. No one said anything to us about how long we would be waiting.

We waited for one hour, and no one came to give an explanation. When I walked into the room to meet the director, he was very laid-back, almost bored. The producer was actually *lounging* on the couch. The vibes were not good.

I think a truly brilliant auditioner could turn that around. I was unable to.

I don't know about what it would be like for you, as a painter. In my field there has to be some seduction. That seduction is easier when you have a partner who would like to be seduced. These people weren't like that. Especially the producer who was lounging, as I say.

I'd love to be a fly on the wall to see which actresses turned them around, and got them to sit up and take notice. I know that it takes a sense of play and fun. In grad school we took clown class. That would have helped. Clowns are always working in relation to authority. Authority is no-nonsense, but the clown is tireless, always trying for, wishing for, approval. It's hard to be a clown. To wish for approval is to make oneself vulnerable. Clowns are tough, ultimately. They have to outsmart the nonchalant ones around them, and at the same time endear themselves to the audience, the ones in charge.

Do you know the painting by the Mexican painter Rufino Tamayo called *The Comedians*? The "comedians" are butchering chickens. I don't know what Tamayo intended, but I have always thought this is a profound painting—pointing to the sacrifice, and sometimes violence, at the base of making art, of being the comedian, the one who is outside and comments back. It's the only position to take in an audition—you have to preserve your outsideness as a platform from which you seduce others, while at the same time you have to do what it takes to get the job.

ADS
Van Nuys, California
March 2004

Audition

Dear BZ:

You asked how I did on my sitcom audition today.

I'm once again sitting in my car (that's often where you will find me in LA), at the Warner Brothers studio lot in Burbank, writing on the BlackBerry. And again—it's hot out here! When you have a job, being on the lot is fun and even romantic. There's so much history; so many movies were made right here. When you don't have a job, it's a drag.

The role I auditioned for was a tough editor of a newsmagazine. My agent just called: "They love you. They think you look great, but they don't think that you are three-camera funny."

They always say "they loved you." No one would talk about doctors, lawyers, salesmen, construction workers, grape pickers that way. We are *workers*. But they talk about love? Between strangers?

So I'm not three-camera funny. On to the next one.

ADS
Burbank, California
March 2004

Your Name/Your Fame

Dear BZ:

Twenty years ago or more, I took a walk on a beautiful beach in New Jersey, and I wrote in the sand: *I have a body. I need a name.* And I took a photograph of that.

It's true. You need a name. More. These days you need a *brand.* People have become *brands.* They are asked to market not just their product but themselves. This is not only true of actors. Surgeons and lawyers become brands. Even human rights activists become brands!

In sports this is clearer than ever. Michael Jordan was labeled as "athlete," and then "brand." Celebrities hire people to think about not just how to get them publicity, but how to attach them to a brand—how to use them to be the "face" for something. And from that they hire specialists to help them conceive of "lines"—of clothing, cosmetics, bedsheets, etc. It's becoming more so by the second. You are entering a generation where artists are full-fledged businesses—probably more than ever in the history of celebrity. (Although I recently read that Shakespeare was a frugal, shrewd entrepreneur who owned a lot of property.) Of course, what lurks is that everyone is in danger of being found out as wearing the emperor's new clothes.

Think of your name—your fame—this way. There is nothing inherently bad or good about the "brand." Connected to the business of making art is the business of becoming better-known. The confusion comes in when we put another type of value on those businesses. Ask yourself: Do you want to become famous in order to fulfill a deeper psychological need?

I tend to avoid pathologizing the things we do as artists. I like to think that we represent certain mythologies—not pathologies. Some psychiatrists believe that artists do what they do to compensate for psychological problems. Many of us have psychological and emotional challenges. That's only part of the story. As artists we bring all of our lives and insights and experiences into our work—but to sum us up with ideas like artists "need attention" or "need to be seen" seems to speak more to the anxiety the viewer has about the attention the artist receives. In fact, I like to think that the artist brings a certain health—and particularly a psychological health and balance—to society, even when the works of art communicate bad news and the darker parts of nature and human nature.

Moreover the need to be heard is not enough. To be heard is only one part of engagement. To develop a voice, you need to develop an ear. To develop a vision you need to develop an eye. To develop your mark as an artist, you need to see the marks of others—especially the marks of those who are unrecognized. Everyone around you is making a mark of some kind.

A woman who worked for the Bush administration addressed a conference I attended a few months after the September 11 tragedy at the World Trade Center in 2001. She talked about "branding" America to get a positive message out to the rest of the world. The conference was filled with businesswomen, and they were enchanted by this idea. But is a "brand" a sufficient public relation, a sufficient mode of diplomacy in the world today? I don't think so. In her confirmation hearing, Condoleezza Rice called for Americans to learn languages and learn about other cultures, other lands. We need to know how to talk and listen and revitalize the art of conversation. A work of art engenders a conversation.

The back-and-forth, sending and receiving, listening and talking, sitting with your pad and paper, or easel, or board and watercolors and watching others watch you paint—all of this can be a kind of leadership, and it can cause change.

ADS
Amagansett, New York
February 2004

Teacher

Dear BZ:

Well, the news is that my television pilot got picked up. At this moment my house is upside down as I pack it up for what might be a month or might be three months or six months or a year, or six years. Such is the life of a television actress. Amazing. The crisis of the day is how to get my dog, Memphis, to LA. The planes have embargos this time of year, because it's too hot to take dogs. I was told by the airlines: Some dogs "succumb" to the heat. That means they die. ("Succumb"—isn't language amazing!) What I've now been told is that I have to hire a service (it will be more expensive to transport my dog than to transport me) and they will drive my dog out on the tarmac in an air-conditioned van and keep her there until the temperature is checked. If it's below a certain level she can get on the plane; if not they take her back to the kennel. This goes on for days early in the morning before it gets hot. My dog is a Diva Dog.

I'm thinking of writing a children's book called *Memphis Goes to Hollywood* to chronicle our life in that town.

But you are the one with the good news. They are going to let you take over a class for two weeks. This is really terrific.

First of all, as discussed briefly on the phone, everything you do with students has to be thought out, as much as possible. It's very important to remember that as a teacher you are not really a "friend," per se. This is a tall order for you.

You're just going into your senior year yourself. But these kids that you are working with from the housing project do have special needs.

Over time friendships develop between teachers and students, students and mentors, but it takes time. The relationship is more formal than a friendship because schools are national and civic institutions. Find a way to be honest and present on the one hand, but create the necessary distance on the other. This is key, and is related to the idea we have explored about being "in it and out of it" at the same time.

A student needs the space/distance to find himself and his work—intellectually especially, and certainly creatively. Creativity is the supreme freedom. It is a freedom that requires discipline and rules, yet it is boundless for the person who taps into it. Your job is to trigger that boundlessness at the same time that you share the rules of your discipline.

A student needs the space to take the lessons given and to develop his/her own independent way of thinking. This is where the tension resides in the relationship. Students project things, too—and you may not even know it. You could be their mother, their father, their sister. You don't have any control over that. You have to acknowledge that it's there and project what you are projecting, but you have to know that what you are sending out could meet a shield coming from the other side. "Projection" is exactly as the word indicates. There you are, and a movie is projected onto your body.

You can start on a pedestal and then find yourself kicked off the pedestal. The opposite happens, too. There are lots of movies about the teacher who had to fight her or his way into the hearts of the students. My personal goal as a teacher is to keep the learning flowing and to make sure that it is not so much about those personal things—or that the relationship, good or fraught, is guided into the most productive interaction possible.

It's funny—probably the best relationship I had with students over the thirty years of my teaching was my last year at Stanford, in my class called Art and Civic Dialogue. Ironically, it was the first time in all my years of teaching that I allowed my students to call me Professor Smith. For years, when a student would call me Professor, I'd say, "Anna is fine." This year I didn't do that. I added a level of formality, and yet I'd say I was closer to that group than to any group I've ever taught.

Teachers have all kinds of styles. Some hang out with students, go shopping with them, have them over to their houses. I've chosen not to go that route. I had a former colleague who went that route and got into a very nasty situation at his university. In teaching art, we are dealing with whole people, their dreams, their passions, their fears. There are not as many boundaries. In other classes the interaction is from the neck up, and certainly there are classes that can be done online. In the arts, however, the real personal interaction is intense and important. Which means that there have to be limits and rules. You have to choose which way makes you most comfortable.

Most of all I'd say the goal is to provide the students with as much space as possible for intellectual and creative development. Space, but highly *organized* space. This is so that there is a structure there for something to happen. I then teach off of what *happens*. I can't anticipate what will happen. I can anticipate, however, that *something* will happen.

Here I am with some of my favorite folks—a bunch of actors rehearsing for my play *House Arrest.*

Kindergarten teachers are my favorite teachers to watch because they have to be organized within an inch of their lives.

ADS
New York City
February 2002

Teacher II

Dear BZ:

So, you got the job to assist the art teacher for the entire summer! This is fantastic news. As to your request for advice about the job:

I am thinking about a wonderful town house I lived in while I was writing my play *House Arrest*. It was actually two houses joined by a garden, and it was turned into a creative space for me by its owners, Priscilla Houghton and her husband, Amo Houghton, a congressman.

A lot of people worked on my project, and they worked very hard. I know that they really enjoyed stopping by the house to talk to Priscilla, who would always have a pitcher of iced tea waiting for them. One of the assistants on the project, Matthew, told me that stepping into Priscilla's house felt like stepping into a "safe haven."

Now, I don't believe in promising students safety. The world is just too rough for that at the moment. I think we should teach resilience. However, having said that, I do think that an assistant teacher—if it's all right with the teacher—can do a lot to make the space in which everyone is working feel solid and pleasing. I think you should think of yourself as a breath of fresh air. Always be very prepared when the students enter the room, so that you can be of service to them; and most important, be *interested* in them. Make a metaphoric garden out of the classroom. (I say this broadly because you really have to back up the style that the teacher has in mind.)

Here are some universals:

Teaching has to do with declaring a space in society—a space that allows for intellectual (or other) inquiry. The way we think of it is "academic freedom." The making of art also requires a space. I do not personally think of that space as a safe space. In this particular civic moment, however, I do think we need to create our classroom as an oasis where different kinds of exploration and creation can happen, where the boundaries are different from what they are in everyday life.

If you become a teacher and ultimately run your own classroom, you will decide what the tone of your classroom is going to be. The point I want to make is that establishing that tone is not "casual." It's something you should think long and hard about, something you should create physically and palpably. It's as important as the exercises, the critiques, the discussion, and all of the other activities in the class.

For example, I always like to place chairs in a semicircle, or a horseshoe, with my chair in the middle when I am addressing the room. When I watch my students perform, I sit either right dead center in the semicircle; or, if the room has been set up with several rows of chairs, I sit in the first row in the center. I strive to be the best audience a student can have, and everyone in the class must also strive to be so.

You should make note on the first day of who is, and who is not, a good audience to the teacher, and who is a good viewer to other students in the class. Some people will sit in a very disinterested way. In the course of time, I actively try to change those people. Body language matters.

So what is the "garden"? How is our classroom different from the other spaces in our students' daily lives? How do we make it evidently and memorably different?

Your boss will tell you what she wants you to do—but it may be interesting for you to read this note that I sent to my assistant teacher, Matthew, a year ago. You will see that I used the garden metaphor with him, too.

- You should always arrive at class before others.
- Try to learn students' names on the first day. SMILE a lot.
- Please organize with the administration in advance of class if we need anything, audiovisual-wise, or otherwise.
- There is a class before us. This is where the garden part comes in. That class will have its own energy, its own vibe, its own leftover coffee cups or whatever.
- I believe that a rehearsal hall, a classroom, a stage is a sacred space.
- You control our space, and provide our garden.
- My favorite thing to do in teaching or directing is to sweep the floor before class or rehearsal starts. For us it's important because we will be working in bare feet. Also, it's important to actually, physically have the image of us taking our space.

So—

- When the class before ours breaks, immediately walk into the room and start to adjust the furniture and sweep the floor. This is a polite signal that they should move into the lobby. It also sets the tone for our work with our students.

- Arrange the chairs. Always set up our chairs in a semicircle, and move any tables out of the way.
- As I recall that room, it has a strange configuration, and maybe even a blackboard. Find the most likely place for the "stage area" and set up the chairs in such a way that the semicircle surrounds and embraces the "stage." I will see it when I come in, and make adjustments—but for now, go in and make your own stab at it.
- Once we are seated, take roll, and make a note if anyone is late.
- I always focus a lot of attention on the least ostentatious person for the first few weeks of school in any class that I do.
- We will need music. Good music. Every week.

In summary, your "making-the-garden" ritual will go like this:

- Wait at the door till the other class breaks.
- Enter.
- Put a CD on.
- Move the furniture, sweep the floor, and arrange the chairs.
- Greet each student by name as he/she enters and take the roll.
- Smile. And make sure you've warmed up before arriving.

The teacher is the landscape architect and will design the class. As assistant, you are the keeper of the garden in any way you are asked to be.

Thanks,

ADS
Taormina, Italy
May 2002

Presence II

Dear BZ:

I'm in Montreal filming *The Human Stain.* It's a wonderful movie based on Philip Roth's novel of the same name. It stars Anthony Hopkins, Nicole Kidman, Ed Harris, and Gary Sinise. It is about a black man who "passes" for white in the 1940s. I play his mother, and the script has a heartrending scene between my son and me, where he comes to tell me that he is going to marry a white woman. When I ask when I will be able to meet her (without going into the fact that this was "just not done," at least not in the 1940s), he informs me that he has told her I am dead.

I spent a lot of time thinking about the scene, of course. On the day of shooting that scene, when I was on breaks, I hid upstairs in a corner of the house that was our set and listened to Schubert's "Ave Maria."

The set was very, very quiet. You could hear a pin drop. Even between cuts, the place was quiet. The director, Robert Benton, who is a very gentle, intense director, set the tone. He loves actors. Which is not always the case with directors, unfortunately. Benton also knows a lot about acting.

Robert Benton has presence—even though for the most part he stands in the back, somewhere behind the camera, or in a corner, and just watches very, very quietly. He is almost invisible. It's almost like he's hiding. He is so intent on the performance—and then he comes out and quietly says something. And what he says is exactly right and exactly on time.

Sometimes presence is invisible, and is only felt. It can cause a good feeling or a bad feeling in a given atmosphere. Benton was all good presence, and it was so creative. Sometimes presence is not in your face. Sometimes presence creates the space in which *you* can be present. I suppose religions manifest the presence, for example, of "the spirit." A place can have presence.

Presence is an invitation.

ADS
Montreal
March 2002

matters of the mind

Questions

Dear BZ:

Okay, as promised, a full report on my interview with the abstract painter Brice Marden.

Yes, he *is* as sexy as you thought. (As to your other questions—Do I think painters have to be sexy? And what does this mean for a woman painter?—I don't have an answer yet. I have to think about those.)

It was so windy outside today that a ferry going to Staten Island crashed and some people died. It was this kind of wind that was howling outside when I interviewed Brice Marden. His studio is in a fairly tall building directly across from the Hudson River in New York City. The studio is stunning—all stone and glass, quite large, two floors. His wife paints on the upstairs level. Some of his paintings were leaning against the stone wall. The vibrant colors really leapt out from the stone.

I asked about Picasso, like you said I should. He dissed the man! Really. In fact, I have transcribed some of the interview for you at the end of this letter, where you'll see that when I asked him about Picasso (and I had in mind what you had said to me, that if you could be anybody, if you could have the talent of anyone, you would pick Picasso) . . . well, he kind of snickered and giggled at the idea of Picasso being idolized. But in the end, he talked about how Picasso did after all make *Guernica*, an incredible, incredible painting—a

Picasso's *Guernica*. It's not just a famous painting, it's one that *asks questions*. When you see it in the Reina Sofía Museum in Madrid, you will see the observers really engaging with it.

"war painting," as he called it. And Marden asks, "Why haven't we made our war painting?"

To me this is the question of our time. "Why haven't we made our war painting?" You know, this morning, in a review of a historical novel about slavery, I came across a reference to Friedrich Engels, who apparently said that he learned more about postrevolutionary France from the novelist Balzac than

from any scholar. You see, this is the possibility we have now. Where is the war painting, where is that work of art that speaks a question to power? Brice asks the question better than I.

Oh, speaking of *questions*. That's another thing. This is critical. It's what we talked about when we met in Denver. I asked Brice what he's looking at when he looks at a painting. You know what he said? He said he's looking for the *questions* that the artist is dealing with, and the way that he deals with the questions. That's really what it's all about. If you take nothing else away from our letters and conversations, that is the single most important idea that you need to take away—curiosity about the questions, respect for the questions, hunger for the questions. And most important, finding your own questions and finding the way to put them into your paintings.

One last thing—as you read the interview, notice what he says about confidence. That's also something you and I have been talking about: Sometimes confidence is overrated! *Questions and uncertainty are the stuff of artists!* Airline pilots need to be confident. The surgeon needs to be confident (but not *too* confident). You need enough confidence to hold your paintbrush, and to show up in the studio, knowing that you are not wasting your time—but after that, I would say uncertainty should prevail. We can never be too sure.

So, on to the interview. The scene: As I say, it was a very windy day. We were on a high floor in this completely stone studio, with very little furniture. He sat by the window in a director's chair, leaning back in it so that the front legs of the chair were off of the floor. He wore black jeans, a black long-sleeved T-shirt with no writing on it. He had reading glasses on a string hanging down his chest, which he picked up every once in a while. He wore tennis shoes. Four of his paintings, each a different color, were to the left of him against the wall.

WAR PAINTING

From an interview with Brice Marden, painter, November 2003

MARDEN
(speaking about Picasso)
But he couldn't do
He couldn't do an abstract painting

He was *Spanish*
He was like based in
He had to deal with things that he *saw*
He was a realist
And it has to do with other ideas that were current
How the physicists were seeing things
So he made this new reality
And then he went on and applied very standard,
Art historical situations to this new
Vision.
He painted the nude,
Endlessly.
And the human
Condition
Endlessly—
In a very pictorial literary way.
I mean I don't want to disparage!
(laughs)
He really isn't one of my favorites!
I mean I kept thinking Cézanne had taken painting to this
point
And he—
Cézanne is talking about, you know, like capturing this
Vision and this *expression* and he's talking about these really
Like very way out there kind of ideas
In this really
Way out there kind of—
And then Picasso comes in and he's really talented
And makes this bunch of mundane paintings!
To me it's Cézanne
You know
And Pollock comes out of Cézanne

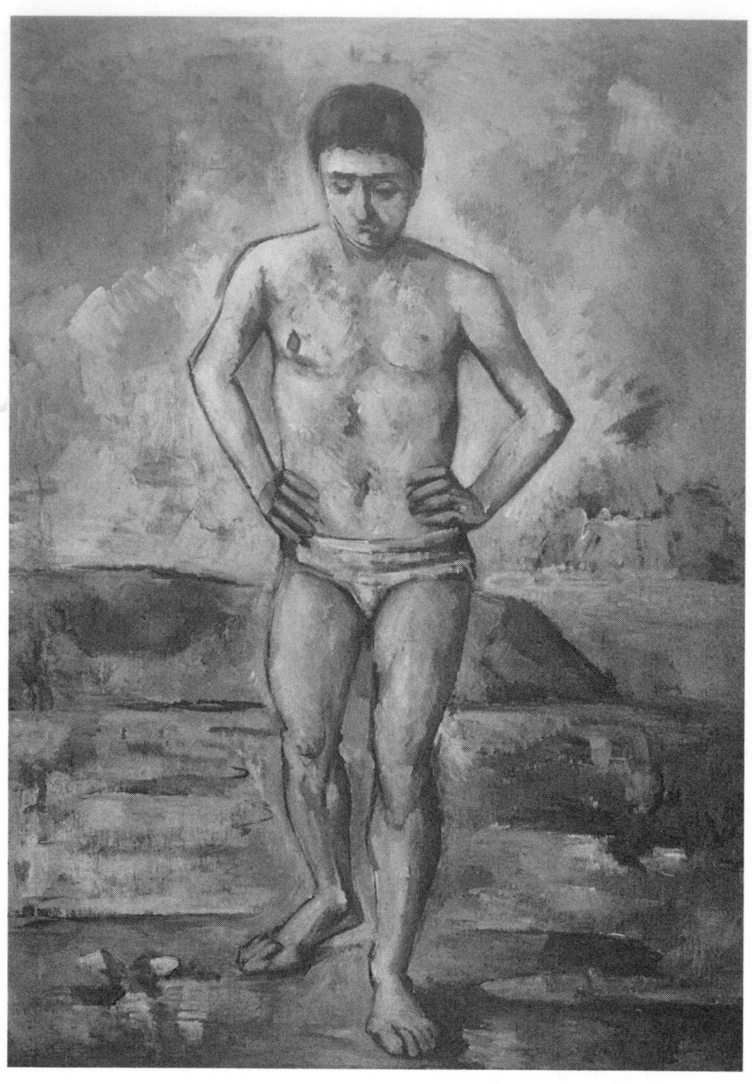

None of us stands alone. We all have influences. Brice Marden was talking about Cézanne's influence on Picasso, and presumably on himself, too. Who are your influences? They've started already!

(Picasso) was really confident
Confidence was a part of it
Which was one of the great things about him
Part of it *is* the struggle just to keep it going.
This sort of intense struggle
Part of it *is* about the struggle
Well I would say—
Confidence
I think part of it
Is the doubt
And the doubt—
It affects the color
Like Picasso
Never doubted that he couldn't draw as well as he wanted to
  draw—
I saw this Gerhard Richter quote
In a Christie's catalog
About how
Abstract painting is this other way of dealing with things
  you just don't know about
Things you can't see
It approaches feelings
In a way
Questioning
It's not a question and answer—
Whereas in a way
A lot of Picasso stuff to me
Is
Or was—
but then again—
I went to see

Guernica
And it's amazing
Really amazing painting
It's like:
"Oh
We haven't done our war painting."
That's the last great war painting.
And how come we haven't done our war painting?
Well
I think
It takes a new understanding
About how horrible it all is
And I think it's coming up
It's gotten so horrible
There's bound to be some insight
Into how horrible it really is.
There can be nuclear war
And the whole thing could just end
And people
I don't think they get that.
That's what
Picasso was reacting to
That sort of
Cold-blooded
Murderous
You know uh
(pause)
The ability to be that way.
And he saw it and reacted to it—
And made thisssss
Unbelievable painting—!
It's really powerful—

Very direct—
You feel the hand going through with a kind of passion—
You know
And it's like this thing—
It's like like the caves—
You see some *bull* on the wall of a cave
And it's there with this kind of
Awe
And you know it's like
The human is in awe of this thing
And because of this awe
They have to make
They have to express
This you know—
And that's the way the *Guernica*—
And we were brought up with it
It was in the Museum of Modern Art,
You'd go see it all the time.
You know
And then suddenly it was gone
And it became an abstraction
And it had lost that meaning
And the meaning's back
When I saw it
Just a couple of weeks ago
It seems to me the meaning's back
And it brings up that question
Why haven't we made our war painting?

ADS
New York City
November 2003

More Than One Idea

Dear BZ:

Today Condoleezza Rice, the National Security Advisor, testified before the 9/11 commission. My interest in her testimony is threefold:

1) I'm concerned about the state of the nation (the nation being the United States).

2) Condoleezza Rice served as provost of Stanford University while I taught there, so she was a former colleague. She attended my performance on one occasion. Now I am having a chance to watch hers.

3) I play the National Security Advisor on *The West Wing*.

Everyone at the gym this morning was crowded around the televisions in the locker room and in the snack bar. The only kinds of shows that draw these kinds of crowds in gyms are important ball games and national disasters (the San Francisco earthquake in the eighties comes to mind—and I'm sure it was so on 9/11, although I did not go to the gym that day).

Everyone spoke about "how she did"—that is, about her performance. Very few people actually discussed the content of her remarks.

Following my visit to the gym I went to a lunch for Brian Williams, who was recently designated lead anchor on *NBC*

Nightly News, set to replace Tom Brokaw when he steps down in December. Again, the performance, not the content, was the subject of most people's remarks. "The only time she seemed to have a rough time was when Richard Ben-Veniste was after her," one person said.

"She was fabulous! Just fabulous," a high-powered black woman in the media exclaimed.

At one point Brian Williams said to me, "I find it interesting that so many people say she's articulate." And he pointed out that the word *articulate* would probably not be used to describe white men in her position. I agree. Why were people commenting that she was "articulate"? She is a highly educated, extremely smart person. It would be like saying of a model, "She's thin." It's beside the point. It goes with the territory. Do people still find it spectacular that a black woman would be articulate? Is it subconscious? Is it still a feat for a black woman to be "articulate"—what was really on display for the American public?

I don't think a black woman in public service has ever been so widely viewed in the history of American politics. Pop stars, yes; stateswomen, no. The last black woman I remember in such a political spotlight was Barbara Jordan, then a young congresswoman from Texas who spoke at the Nixon impeachment hearings. BZ, I wish you could hear how Barbara Jordan sounded. You can find it in libraries. It was not only a political moment; it was a moment in the history of rhetoric in this country. It was a perfectly written, perfectly performed rhetorical event that did help change the course of history. After all, rhetoric is the foundation of political life. The powers of persuasion are essential to who wins and who loses. Is the only way for us to learn what happened prior to

9/11 through the discourse of persuasion? Aren't we searching for the truth? But rhetorical power is what shapes history, if not truth.

There is no forum out of which we can discuss and learn about security that is not partisan. And in this case, unlike other issues that have been a part of our political lexicon, our lives and the lives of people all over the world, of every age, race, and creed, are at stake.

When asked why he chose to be a playwright rather than a statesman, the absurdist French playwright Eugène Ionesco answered, "Because as a playwright I can have more than one side, more than one idea."

Now is the time for artists to create—with their work, and with their audiences—a forum where we can speak about survival outside of the context of party politics. And we should inspire our public to demand of our political leaders that they too help create that forum.

ADS
New York City
April 8, 2004

Art and Reality

Dear BZ:

I don't normally engage in conversations about things like, "What's the difference between art and reality?" But I'm intrigued that you ask the question.

First, a caution. I think of art as *work,* so I worry about going off into the stratosphere with theoretical questions like, "What is art? What is truth?" (See the Gospels in the Bible and a discussion by Pontius Pilate just before Jesus Christ was crucified if you want some real art on the theme of truth, for example.) If we get caught up in pondering these questions, we sell ourselves short. How we live, and how we treat one another, is what is at issue.

Although such questions suggest ideals, or perfections, or states of normalcy, or even states of excellence, a close look will show us that everything is corrupted by our limitations as human beings. The difference between art and reality is simple. You know the answer. But maybe you're asking me if all of reality is a kind of art, since it has to do with perception. I teach in the performance studies department at my university. My colleagues expand the idea of what performance is to include many things that you might call everyday life.

You should read some real philosophers on the relationship of art to reality. There are learned people who hold art in relatively low estimation. Some psychiatrists, for example, think of art as a way of dealing with neurosis. It pleases me to note that art has been around a lot longer than Western European psychiatry, and from the looks of where psychiatry is going—to pharmaceuticals—I feel very confident that art will be around a lot longer, neurosis or not.

Perhaps art is a quest for the perfect, or even the imperfect. Reality always falls short on both sides. For that matter so does art, depending on who the observer is. You might think that Picasso is as close to perfection as one could get. Someone else may disagree. I may think that *A Raisin in the Sun* is a wonderful play, and someone else, back when it was first produced, thought it was disrespectful to black men and a sellout of the black community. Someone else thinks Elvis Presley is the best thing that ever came out of America, and maybe I don't get it. Someone else likes Britney Spears, and you may think: Are you out of your mind? You call that art? And onward we go. You see, all the observers are human beings without perfection, because by nature we are stuck with human limitation, and above all we are imprisoned by our own subjectivity.

Years ago I studied at a conservatory in San Francisco, and I would climb an incredibly steep hill to an extraordinary cathedral, Grace Cathedral, and take Holy Communion every day. I would then go down the hill to swim. Every day. And then home for a pauper's breakfast, and then into the studios for voice and diction exercises. Every day. I was really into "doing." Many of my classmates loved to talk and ponder (on themes like "art and reality"). But I didn't see it improving their acting. In those days it was still considered all right to smoke and drink well into the night, although the beginnings of the "health nut" phase were approaching. I don't think there was bottled water yet, but we did wear special shoes for posture, and many of us were vegetarian—although most of us were so poor that we'd eat whatever we could get for free.

I began to think that, as I've said earlier, talking about acting was like thinking about swimming. I could sit on the end of the lap lane and ponder swimming, or I could jump in and day after day increase my stamina. I could attempt to perfect my stroke, only to realize that I have certain physical limitations that would inhibit it. I've been swimming for twenty-eight years and my kick is still pathetic, but my stroke is much stronger than it was when I was younger. Even though I did not become a world-class swimmer, I did teach myself some things about discipline, and I increased my stamina physically. I also increased my mental stamina and my patience.

With that cautionary preface, I'll go ahead and say some things about my own thoughts on the difference between art and reality, if you'll promise that, for as long as you sit with your friends and ponder such questions as the difference between art and life, you'll spend at least the same amount of time painting!

My very smart friend Chula has what I think is an imaginative idea about art. She uses the expression "the economy of art." Art is, above all, economical. By that I mean that it both condenses and amplifies the world. Shakespeare wrote of loves and wars, of kingdoms building, of kingdoms falling, of human frailties and passions in a limited number of lines and a limited number of rhythmic beats, a limited number of actors, a limited number of effects—in fact, very few effects, and no real horses, ships, or taverns. Art is always essentially more economical than reality. Even the lushest movie set is not as lush as reality.

As an artist, part of your gift is to see the world from a distance. I call it a "necessary distance." I take that expression from the photographer Mary Ellen Mark, who wrote in the preface of her book of photographs *American Odyssey* that the camera gave her the way to get close to strangers, but it also provided the "necessary distance."

As artists standing on the outside of that which passes us by, distant from that which is around us, we begin to make another "version" of life. This version, this artifact or representation, is, first of all, fixed. Life is not. Life keeps changing. But so far, at least, art has something about it that remains fixed. I imagine that could change. And indeed, some artists create works that are meant to be affected by life. Yet the parameters are fixed by a concept. Art has a concept. Life does not, unless you believe in spiritualities that see our lives as concepts manifest by God or gods.

Even in improvisation, for example, there is some central theme upon which the artist descants each time he or she produces or performs. Art has a frame; it has a form. I don't know if life, or reality, has such a frame. There is order to how we are as living organisms, but is there a frame? Some would say yes. Others would say it's random.

The real question is, why do you ask the question?

Art is more than a representation of life. It is more than a mirror. It is more than a snapshot. The photographer sets up lights, uses shutter speeds, etc., to make a "likeness," which is as much about his/her eye as it is about what is observed. Did you happen to see the cover of *Vanity Fair* where the photographer Annie Leibovitz photographed President George W. Bush and his defense team the winter after the World Trade Center was hit by terrorist planes? That is not just a photo—not just a mirror. The photographer is creating a sort of fiction out of this group of people. Yet art strives to make meaning.

They say that art should stand the test of time. Life lasts a limited amount of time. Mountains and trees and earth will outlive human beings, but we don't know if they will be here always. Art does outlast the life span of its maker. Art should communicate to an increasing circle of strangers—people who do not know the artist, but come to know the work, and through the work, come to know something about the humanity of the artist that rings with their own humanity.

Art is a product, a fixed thing, that ultimately stands apart. (One wonders: How could the same person who wrote *In Cold Blood*, Truman Capote, write such warm Christmas tales, or even *Breakfast at Tiffany's*, for that matter?) On the other hand, part of what sells movies is the incredible publicity machine that keeps the American public (and now, the world) addicted to learning about the intimate details of the lives, loves, and scandals of movie stars. We say the personal life of an artist should not matter. But it does, to the business of selling the art.

An artist is a public figure, yet rarely is an artist asked to take as much responsibility for what he says behind the mask of art as a politician or an activist might take for saying something much less provocative. And when an artist is asked to take responsibility for provocative images or expressions, we become concerned that it may be a form of censorship. So already it is assumed that in art there is more room for "expression" than there is in "reality." You might be able to make a cartoon in which you would make your teacher appear to be an idiot. Yet you would be more likely to get away with that than if you went in front of the teacher, in reality, and called her/him an idiot. You might cause a controversy by the cartoon, but in the United States, it's unlikely you would be expelled from school for it.

On Sunday I went to the Whitney Museum in New York City to see an exhibit of the work of Jacob Lawrence. I had traveled to Seattle, Washington, to meet with him twice before his death. He was in his eighties, and frail. He was humble and wise, and everything he said to me was rendered so simply, so economically. Perhaps we could say that any life well-lived would lead one to a kind of economy of expression that my friend Chula was talking about. It was with great anticipation that I approached the Whitney, as this would be the first time I would see Mr. Lawrence's paintings "for real," as it were.

I was surprised that about an hour after the museum's opening, the line was around the block. It was moving to me to be among a more diverse crowd than is usual at artistic events. There were people of all colors, of all ages, and from abroad as well as from the United States. Everyone walked slowly around the exhibit of his *Migration Series*, painting by painting. These simple pictures, which represented various stages of the migration of "Negroes, as they were called, from the Southern U.S. to the North," all added up to something that was a very eloquent testament to the power of the Negro quest for dignity, good living conditions, joy, work, peace.

An artist is a collector of life's moments, a memorizer of its images. Yet art is always much more than the sum of its parts. It always gets right to our souls; it gets right to our core values—values we didn't even know we had. It brings out the best in us, and people fear that it could bring out the worst and could *cause* the worst. It's extraordinary that people get confused between what they see and what really is, and here your question—"What's the difference between art and reality?"—has a different resonance. In other words, if I believe the violence I see in a movie has no more consequence than it does in a movie, and I then commit such an act, have I confused art and reality? Does art then dangerously affect reality?

We either resonate toward or away from the artist's ability to communicate right straight through to each of us, even as we are often "strangers." Art creates community. It doesn't necessarily unify, but it creates community out of a disparate bunch of people who happen to observe the same thing, especially when they view the same thing at the same time. It can help us feel our humanness. In the summer of 1980, when I was a dog walker living in a fifth-floor walkup in New York City, I shared a cab from JFK airport back into Manhattan with two women who had flown in from Brazil to see the Picasso retrospective. It was exhilarating to observe the *size* and variety of Picasso's community. And the museum was *packed*.

Does reality do all of that? Of course it can. But it usually takes extraordinary circumstances in life for that to happen, or a certain shift in point of view, so that you, as observer, are observing life in a new way, just one step away from it. You are not only a participant in the daily affairs of your life, but you are also reflecting. And if that happens, is it art? No, because art requires more than the ability to step back. It requires discipline, ability, concentration, talent, a variety of perceptive abilities as well as motor skills to create another product, a thing. It requires that you make something else exist that is a representation of what your feeling is. Or your idea. Take, for example, one of my favorite songs—"Stand" as sung by gospel singer BeBe Winans. I listen to it and become spellbound. So much so that my dog comes over to me to see what's going on. What could bring that about? What did it take to bring that about? A combination of skills and discipline and great feeling. "*What-do-you-do-when-you've-done-all-you-can? You just stand,*" he sings.

I just saw the tap dancer Savion Glover doing improvisation with a jazz band. His body was like a musical instrument. He was striving to metamorphose his body, out of his body into something else. A young man, he seemed to carry the wisdom of the ages with his steps. That's *defying* reality.

ADS
Ohio State University
Columbus, Ohio
Spring 2005

matters of the heart

Fear

Dear BZ:

You ask about fear. I take fear seriously. It would be easy to say, "Oh, there's nothing to be afraid of," but I think that's a little disingenuous.

One of the things I loved the most about the period in which I was becoming an artist is that the people around me—the teachers, the mentors—took seriously things that previously in my life had been brushed aside. I remember being terrified of yoga class on the first day, because I learned that we'd have to stand on our shoulders and on our heads, and do all kinds of risky-looking bends. I stayed after class and waited till everyone had left and said to the teacher, "I don't think I'll ever be able to do this. I'm afraid of standing on my head." She didn't smile, which scared me more. She just looked at me very directly and said calmly, "I think it's more about learning a movement." I was similarly terrified of circus class because we had to hang upside down from a trapeze. I told the circus teacher that I was afraid of heights. She said, "I understand fear. Fear is real. I respect fear."

First of all, don't deny fear. It's a feeling like all feelings. Sometimes it is there as a warning. Sometimes you don't need the warning and sometimes you do. Work through fear until your body—or your psyche—gets a better idea of what you can do, until it gets a better idea that you don't need the warning.

But here's a truth about acting that probably applies to a lot of other kinds of artistic performances: There is a way that you are more fragile, emotionally and psychologically, when you are preparing to be onstage and when you are onstage, than you are in real life. The whole "culture of backstage" may be a way of dealing with that. The sort of bedroom atmosphere of the diva's dressing room, for example—all the flowers, gifts, photographs, etc.—are there to condition you and help give you stamina. The fragility is a real thing. Mean-spirited people with no sense whatsoever that one could have actual "fragility" about their work make all sorts of jokes and remarks about people doing the work: "She's being a diva" is their favorite put-down phrase. And the fact is that we all proceed to do something that requires tremendous physical, intellectual, and vocal strength in that very same state of fragility. Both are required; both are present.

Few people understand this. Most just want to get you to produce—and you have to be aware of that because nothing's going to change it. So you have to be very strong, and very able to stand on your own two feet. This notion of knowing who you are, knowing where you stand, knowing what you think is right, knowing how to fight for what you think is right, knowing how to be centered, and knowing where your moral core is, will be the thrust of all I ever write to you. Not the fragility. Fragility is a given. My goal is to teach you how to work with your fragilities, how to be a force with them, how to lead with them, and how to bring others around to their moral center and how to get others to do what's right. Otherwise people will take advantage of that perceived sensitivity and fragility and do ridiculous and sometimes hurtful things to you. You can see this played out with very famous people all the time.

Many great performers have fear. Some take prescription drugs to lower their anxiety level. My theory is that sometimes you just go on some kind of overload, and that causes the fear, or the fright. I read that late in his career, when he was already thoroughly established and recognized as one of the greatest living actors, Laurence Olivier had such terrible fear that someone had to stand in the wings in his view while he was onstage.

I'm not sure if your fear is this kind of fear. Your fear sounds a little more like uncertainty. Is it a lack of courage? The life of an artist is risky: There's a lot to be afraid of. Poverty, no health insurance, no dignity when you can't find work, dealing with people at every level who are thinking of you as a commodity—or worse, people ignoring you, people not believing in you, dismissing your work. The supreme danger is that you could be invisible. But the fact is, you have to be stronger than all of that. I'd suggest you spend your time building up your strength rather than "worrying" about what the life of an artist might bring. You will need extraordinary physical, intellectual, emotional, spiritual strength. You can find story after story—you know them all; gossip columns are full of them—of performers who have been betrayed, stolen from, you name it. Some of this, of course, is just gossip-column stuff, but the fact is that it's very important to have mental clarity and clarity of personal purpose. Clarity about who you are. And even if you decide not to be an artist—even if you change your mind and become a banker, let's say—you will need that clarity and independence. You will need the ability to know what you think is right and wrong, and the ability to stand for something. I have to tell you, BZ, you're sounding a little namby-pamby lately. You need a center. And there's no time like the present to start to work on that for yourself.

Most important is the health and strength of your imagination, which must thrive. Clear away all obstacles and doubts. I don't know a single artist at any level who has faced a life without fear, or without challenges. Remember my swimming metaphor: Just get in and swim your laps. Build your stamina. You will need it. Believe me, no matter how successful you are, you will need it.

Be strong, be new, be you.

ADS
Los Angeles

Sense Memory

Hi, BZ:

Your grandmother is losing her memory. Her short-term memory, that is. She cannot remember seeing you yesterday, but she can remember with clarity her girlhood. I would like to take this interest that you have in memory and talk about your memory as a gold mine for your art.

My aunt Esther said to me, about two years before she died, "Old age is sad; nobody tells you it's going to be this sad." And she looked at me with her clear gray eyes. And it broke my heart.

So: memory. Memory is not only a practical utility that helps us know where we are. Memory is an essential substance for us, as artists. Memory is the beginning of romance; it's at the root of feeling. We are a conglomerate of complicated memories, all kinds of memories that make us who we are. Now, your grandmother can't remember that you came to see her yesterday, and she certainly can't remember what you gave her for her birthday, but she can remember her fifth birthday party. And possibly she longs for that.

My favorite quotation—or let's say the quotation that really gets to *why* I have chosen to be an artist:

"A man's work is nothing but this slow trek to rediscover, through the detours of art, those two or three great and simple images in whose presence his heart first opened."

That is a passage from Albert Camus. I learned it from

a remarkable man named Barney Simon. I met Barney in Johannesburg, South Africa, in the summer of 1994, just after black South Africans got the vote for the first time. Barney ran a theater called the Market Theater, which had been an important part of bringing apartheid down. And the theater, by the way, was named for an interesting reason. This is a tangent, but bear with me. In South Africa it was illegal for blacks and whites to assemble together in groups. So this theater, the Market Theater, was dedicated to ending apartheid—it was a political theater. As such, its audience had to be mixed. What good would it do to have it speak only blacks to blacks or whites to whites? It was a theater about bringing humans together. But it kept getting closed down, because it was illegal to assemble blacks and whites together. So then they found a space in downtown Johannesburg in an old marketplace. As they were about to be shut down again, someone pulled up from the dustiest of annals some old, ancient law that allowed blacks and whites to assemble in the marketplace. Since the theater was situated on land that had been a market, they were allowed to continue.

So for me, this quotation from Camus—both what it says, and how I came upon it—says it all. My work is nearly a full-time enterprise of trying to reach back and find those great and simple images that first found access to my heart.

Being an artist requires an intense identification of all aspects of life. For acting, this requires an ability to experience, absorb, accept, feel, and transmit all aspects of the human condition—all notes on the scale. It is exactly this "rediscovery" with open arms, of all of those elements, in the way that they first found access to my heart. Some of them made my heart sing, some of them held my heart like a cradle, some made my heart tremble, others made my heart break. But it's all part of it. BZ, you can also help others rediscover those two or three great and simple images through your work.

ADS

Soul

Dear BZ:

Today I went to talk to a group of high school students. One of them asked me what "acting" was. This is what I said:

"Acting is the ability to believe that you are someone else: that you could be in someone else's shoes. It is the ability to create with your body an image of that person that resonates through your attempt to *feel* as that person. It is making a character out of an idea or out of language, and presenting that character to an audience in such a way that the people in the last row of the peanut gallery feel as if you are standing right next to them. Or it's presenting your character in a way that leaps right off the screen and into a person's skin, or into the bottom of their belly and into their hearts. It's making them think about your character as if you were real, or out of a powerful dream, the next day, or weeks later. It's making them feel as if they have really spent time with you, and that something intimate has happened. Sometimes the feeling is more powerful than the feelings they have about people in their real lives, whom they think they have intimacy with but they don't. Acting is managing to have intimacy even in a complicated and frightening world, where most of us want only to protect ourselves from one another, and certainly we want to protect ourselves from strangers. Acting is magic because in fact you are a stranger to a stranger, and in a brief amount of time you make yourself familiar.

"Sometimes actors are not engaging or even interesting people. Commerce tries to make them seem engaging and interesting, and wants to project that intimacy so that you will buy things with that person's face or name or words. In other words, you will buy more time with them. It's the chemistry between them and you that is interesting, not them alone. It's the whole bundle—the actors in their costumes, and with music behind them, that is interesting. Obviously the actor is a compelling part. As humans we are interested in seeing the human face of things, and acting puts a human face on things or on deep feelings or on ideas. Acting is bridging the gap between yourself and the character, yourself and the playwright, yourself and the director, yourself and the other actors, yourself and the costume, yourself and the light, yourself and the objects, yourself and the actions. Acting is bridging the gap between the character and the audience, yourself and the audience. Acting is going into a dark place, whether a theater or a soundstage, or a bright place, and exposing your *soul* to a group of strangers, whether three or thirty, whether in a movie theater or a live theater, on a street corner or an ocean liner."

One boy in the class, who was wearing a sweater vest and suit coat, said, "Do you really think it's exposing your *soul*?" And he emphasized the word *soul*. I said, "Of course."

ADS
New York City

Empathy

Dear BZ:

I just came from a long, memorable, and rather amazing day, with some bizarre tones to it.

I can't remember if I filled you in on my most recent project. I have been up here at Yale University at the medical school as a visiting professor. I have been interviewing doctors and patients, and then I performed (the patients and doctors for the doctors) at something called medical grand rounds. Now, medical grand rounds are usually a pretty stuffy affair, where an expert delivers a lecture in an old amphitheater at the medical school. I had decided that if I was going to dare take acting into this place, I'd better just go all the way.

I had to perform at eight in the morning. It was slightly terrifying—going in and facing all those white coats, starched shirts, and perfect ties. There were women there, too—but the character of the place is still very male, and very old. And for their side of it, I hear they were a little miffed at having to turn off their pagers as they came into the amphitheater.

As it turned out, they were blown away. They gave a thunderous standing ovation, tears were shed, and . . . well, I did what I came to do. Surgically almost.

But let me put in this tangent before going on. Word was out that I was there. There were very limited seats. And some students from the drama school had wanted to come to my morning performance. Now, I was going to be giving another performance for the general public the next day—but some of them were determined to come to the one with the doctors. Perhaps they had rehearsals or classes that conflicted the next day. There was not enough room to accommodate them in the amphitheater itself, so the medical school suggested having a video feed into another room, where they could watch. Nonetheless a group of them somehow sneaked into the medical amphitheater, and tried to literally "hide"—it was a very small space—or at least to be incognito with their scarves wrapped around their necks and faces. I loved this, because it's exactly this clan, really this family of artists that you meet everywhere in the world, this intensity, this desire to see something new—to be with something new. Years ago, when I first lived in New York, I would go to bars where progressive jazz was being played just to watch the musicians who came and stood way in the back. I liked to watch them watch the music. So, in the midst of these doctors are the actors incognito, and I felt that they were rooting for me in their clandestine way.

That was just the beginning of the day! After that, I had to go to classes of students at the school at all levels, and at the end of the day, after dinner, I met with the third-year students from the medical school and the graduate students at the drama school. Now this is what was bizarre.

That night after dinner, all of us paraded into this huge, huge wooden library at Yale. Dark brown wood, and just huge and high. And there were chairs lined up on either side of an aisle. I was introduced to the audience of students by a wonderful doctor named Gerald Friedland, who is a major name in the treatment of AIDS. He has been involved with treating AIDS patients for many years, long before it became a publicly known disease and long before AIDS became a part of our vocabulary and our culture. When I got up to speak, the first thing I noticed was that the doctors were seated on one side, and the artists on the other. Now how could I tell?

By their dress. But *also*—now this is interesting, because this is purely subjective; this is not factual, but this is how we make realities, from our subjective experiences—in my mind's eye, I have an image of that huge, dark, wood-paneled room. On one side there was a small crowd. The medical student who sticks most in my mind was a slightly heavyset, open-faced, friendly-looking white man in his twenties, with clean, short, light brown hair, wearing a blue blazer and a striped shirt that was open at the neck. He was sort of sitting back, with one ankle resting on his other knee. On the other side was a small crowd, and the student who sticks out in my mind was an African-American woman sitting in the front row, with a notebook and a look of intensity and excitement on her face, like she was poised to ask a question. She was not sitting back at all.

Now which side do you think the doctors were on, and which side were the actors on? The actors were on the side where the black woman was, and the doctors were on the side where the guy in a blue blazer and a short haircut was. It would be a different world if it were the other way around.

So this session began with the African-American woman, asking her question, pen in hand, but nearly in tears before she even began to speak.

"Professor Smith," she said. "Excuse me, but I just . . . Oh excuse me." And she broke down crying. "Excuse me for being so emotional, but I was reading today something that James Baldwin wrote about the terror and the pain of being an artist. . . ." She cried again. "And I was wondering if you could say something about that terror and pain."

Before speaking I glanced across the room at the young medical residents, all fully composed, people who dealt with death every day. And I looked over at the artists.

At one point the open-faced young white man raised his hand and very calmly talked about being a pediatrician, and about what it was like to tell a parent that a child was dying. And about how for the children it's not as difficult as it is for the parents.

And I marveled at the composure of the doctors as they discussed real life, real terror, real pain, real death—and the emotion of the artists as they talked in metaphor.

But this is the very thing that makes me love artists so much. The heart. The soul. The lack of composure. The mess. The image that was given to me of the long-haired student wrapped in her scarf trying to be incognito among the doctors in their white coats, at eight A.M.

I just love 'em. Wouldn't it be nice if the actors had some of the scientific distance of the doctors? Wouldn't it be nice if the doctors had some of the empathy of the actors?

ADS
Yale School of Medicine
New Haven, Connecticut

Stage Fright

Dear BZ:

So you have to present an award to a painter who is visiting your school, and you say you have stage fright.

But is this real stage fright? Or are you just a little nervous in anticipation? The more prepared you are, the more that will diminish. However, regardless of how prepared you are, the moment you walk out and face the crowd, you may feel overwhelmed, as if you have nothing of value to say, as if the words won't come forward, and as if everyone you are facing is wiser than you. Well, those things are not true, of course. So the first thing to realize about stage fright, of any sort, is that it is not grounded in reality.

I am always amazed at the people who face thousands without having any of the signs of nerves—sweat, shaking hands, trembling voices. Politicians, for example. They can't afford nerves. What would we think of a president who was trembling while he gave the State of the Union? I think that they must have so much lust for the crowd that it outweighs any other anxiety. This idea of the lust for the crowd is key. But this lust is tricky. It is not always apparent.

On the surface, you may think you dread the crowd, even hate the crowd. Many people are very conflicted about this. My suspicion is, the greater that conflict, the more unresolved it is, the greater the chance of behaviors and habits that are not useful in the long run. Not to sound like an absolute fuddy-duddy, but this is where sex, drugs, and alcohol often come into the picture.

There are rock stars who take beta-blockers and other drugs to deal with stage fright. To go out and face thousands, as rock stars do, or for you to face several hundred people *should* cause anxiety! It's not natural for everyone.

It ought to be simple—"I want to draw for you." And the "you" gets larger. "I want to sing for you," and the "you" gets larger. "I want to dance for you," and the "you" gets larger. But as the "you" gets larger, things get more complicated. Number one, you are in commerce, as the "you" gets larger. Number two, you are in competition with others, as the "you" gets larger. Number three, more and more people want to say something about who you really are or are not, as the "you" gets larger—and what they say may or may not have anything to do with you. And there's a number four and a number four hundred and a number four thousand. It's complicated to have something to show, or to say, and then have people love it or hate it.

So your feelings about who "you" are in all this can get complicated, too. Case in point: A world-renowned painter is coming to your school, and a number of people could have been chosen to introduce him, but *you* are the one they chose. If someone other than you had been chosen, you might have been envious of their position. You are the one who gets to meet the guest, to go to lunch with him, to stand backstage with him. An honor. Even so, you tell me you have "stage fright." Perhaps it's only excitement, anticipation, as I say—like having your heart race when someone you love is getting off a plane and you haven't seen them in a long time. But since you bring the term *stage fright* into our discussion, I'll take you at your word for the moment.

There are psychologists and psychiatrists who know more about this than I do, but here are a few thoughts. To deal with stage fright, you have to first and foremost know how you tick—how you work, how your body and your mind react. Your body lets loose a lot of adrenaline when you face others, because you are about to communicate on a higher level. I asked the great opera singer Jessye Norman about it. Her attitude is, "If anyone out there can do better than I, then just step right up!" What a terrific attitude, if you can muster that up. For myself, I learned that to be onstage requires a specific discipline, a specific lifestyle. I control what I eat and drink: no caffeine, no alcohol, etc. When I'm performing, I do not take phone calls or have meetings after three P.M. I go to the theater early. I meet with a vocal coach and do a vocal warm-up, or do one on my own. I do relaxation exercises. I take more time with myself than I would take, I suspect, if I were going to my job on Wall Street, or in a law firm, or even in a hospital.

I think that it's quite a challenge to face strangers all the time—large groups of them, which is what we do—and to face them potentially with the most intimate parts of ourselves, and to presumably reach those parts of an audience. Athletes, by the way, have taken sports psychology very seriously. Some believe that once they are at a winning level, then winning is 95 percent psychological and 5 percent physical. I would say that a lot of the psychology of those of us who dare to find the familiar in what is the strange, huge diversity of the human race—to presume to be able to speak to each person in our public, in our audience, through our work, as if we were close to them—requires a psychological adjustment. Just as the athlete must truly believe he or she can win, and truly ignore anything that gets in the way, truly concentrate, so we have to truly believe that what we are presenting belongs in the view of others. Somewhere we must believe that, even if it is not conscious.

How do we take away the strangeness? How are we able to stay connected to our center, to our self-knowledge in circumstances that threaten to take our focus away?

Stage fright is about being with people who are strangers. To deal with stage fright you have to deal with your ideas about strangeness, *and* alienation.

It is a two-sided fear. It is a fear of being *visible* in front of others. It is also a fear of being *invisible* or *becoming invisible* in front of others.

Stage fright is about the possibility that your own authority will vanish in the face of the power of others. This, I think, is at the crux of stage fright. Whatever you can do to establish your authority ahead of time, you should do. Go early to the venue—walk around the audience, walk around the stage—so that the place itself does not seem strange. Performers always do sound checks and light checks to be prepared to have *authority* over the space.

Stage fright is about losing focus.

Spend the night before, and most of the day, getting focused. To achieve this I personally shut down my world the closer I get to performance. There are others who do the opposite—some people just make going onstage an extension of whatever they happen to be doing. Years ago, I went to see Bill Cosby backstage between shows. I was with someone who knew him well, and so he asked us to sit down. He talked nonstop, telling stories for the entire hour or so between shows. Then he got up from his seat in his dressing room and walked out onstage, just as if it were simply a continuation of the conversation backstage, which he was now having with strangers. Yet all that time backstage with us, I believe he was doing a form of focusing.

Stage fright can be fought by whoever can tell you that everything is all right.

This is what friends are for.

When I was in Washington, D.C., performing my play *Twilight: Los Angeles, 1992*, the phone rang in my hotel room one Saturday afternoon. It was someone from the Ford's Theater telling me that President Clinton was planning to come to see me perform the next day. I hung up the phone. My first reaction was not—as I have suggested it should be—"Fantastic! The president of the United States, the first lady, and the vice president are coming to the theater. I have a lot to say to them that I've wanted them to hear! I can't wait!" That was not my reaction. My reaction was not that of one of the young actors in the Broadway play *A Member of the Wedding*, who, when the stage manager announced, "Places," went skipping up and down the hallways backstage, knocking on dressing room doors gleefully calling out, "It's time! It's time!"*

My reaction was the opposite. My friend Jane, who I've known since I was sixteen years old, happened to have dropped by the hotel and was there when the call came. I mumbled, "Clinton is coming to the show." Suddenly all my voice, all my confidence, was gone. And yet I had nearly three

---

* As recounted by actess Elaine Stritch in her one-woman show *Elaine Stritch at Liberty*.

hours' worth of text prepared to say, a show that I had done all over the country and been awarded for. Not to mention the fact that many people had campaigned to get the president to come to my show. So why didn't it feel like a victory?

My goal here is not to psychoanalyze myself in this letter—but just to point out that one possibility is that we may actually both *long for and dread* the audience. And ultimately it is your *joy*, your desire to be in their presence, even if you dread it up until the moment you are literally shoved on to the stage—it is your *joy* (even if you are not conscious of it, or your passion, or your rage) that must push you out there. Basically, you have to want to show it, want to say it, in spite of the fact that psychologically—having nothing to do with reality—you dread it.

My friend Jane was the perfect person to hear my dread. She listened, which is often what friends can do best—allow you to hear yourself, in the ridiculousness of yourself.

As it turned out, I had no stage fright at all in the presence of the president. Possibly because there were too many real things that threatened to take away my concentration. I arrived at the theater and the place was lined with Secret Service. My stage manager called the show with SWAT team guys carrying guns standing in the booth. The audience was pumped up. They laughed harder than usual, and even called things out to the stage. I realized *they were performing* for Clinton, too—and so I was occupied with riding a different type of audience, of being almost in a circus, with Secret Service lining the walls, and the audience performing as much as I was.

BZ, I've said a lot more than you need to know as you prepare to introduce this painter to your student body. Be prepared. Write a nice introduction, one that informs the audience and excites them about your guest, one that makes the guest feel welcome, and one that *you* are excited to deliver. Get the list of his awards right, fact-check everything, and personalize it with what it means to you to have him there. After all, BZ, I'm assuming that you'll get a Nobel Prize or something comparable—might as well start now, knowing that what you are doing is something that people want to see. It won't bode well if your hands shake in Stockholm.

ADS

keeping the faith

Chains

Dear BZ:

A wonderful young artist named Lyle Ashton Harris, who works in the medium of photography, has e-mailed me a request to write the catalog copy for a new exhibition. It is the most interesting work—he has dressed himself as Billie Holiday and taken photographs of it. He has also taken photographs of himself as a boxer. It's very moving. I am writing the text now. I think I'm going to call it "Lookin' for Daddy," which is what he tells me Billie Holiday is all about. I'll try to see if I can get one of the images to you. The boxing images are my favorite, since I've started boxing for exercise. Anyway, Lyle is an interesting artist, and you should know about him.

Interesting, too, that in your last e-mail you wanted to discuss racial and social barriers. Lyle is African-American, and his work addresses race and gender in one of the most imaginative ways I've seen in any art form.

But your question about race and social barriers is: Do they get in the way of people's art? No. People's race, class, gender, family background can't keep them from being artists or from expressing themselves. Expression comes from inside.

There are things about race, social class, gender, family background that could cause some obstacles to expression. I have met people who literally have no expression on their faces, regardless of what happens to them, and people who have absolutely no vocal variety regardless of what happens. This amazes me, because small babies have a multitude of

This is a photo by Lyle Ashton Harris, who experiments with identity by actually posing as the kinds of figures he is exploring in his art. Here he's a boxer. (In the same exhibition he photographed himself as the singer Billie Holiday.)

expressions and melodies, as do young children. And of course, we tend to associate certain kinds of expressions with cultures. Stereotypically the English are not expressive, but the Italians are. Nonetheless, even if you come from the most repressive environment imaginable, you still can have a range of expression. To be an artist, one must have a wide expressive range and a profound desire to communicate. That desire to communicate has to be larger than the chains that bind.

There are so many chains to break out of, chains that come from our inhibitions about a multitude of things:

- how we look, how we sound: Do we look and sound stupid?
- chains from poverty, in the event that one of us came from poverty—never feeling as though we can fill the hole created by that disadvantage
- chains from wealth, in the event that one of us is wealthy—being in the shadow of our wealthy father, or mother, or sister, or ancestor
- chains from religious beliefs
- chains because of racial prejudice
- chains because of expectations about the presentation of oneself in gender and expressions of sexuality
- chains from our friends, or from families who'd rather that we not have a strong will to communicate
- chains from fear

It could go on and on. The chains are real.

But the pure fact of the matter is that art defies the real. The ballet dancer seems to have jumped ten feet when she has jumped only five. Over time it hurts to jump; she jumps in spite of the pain, in defiance of the pain. Art defies the real; it does not reiterate the real. Your passion must be greater than your chains or you cannot create art.

African slaves in the United States sang songs in the fields, and a form of music evolved over time. Human beings want to defy their chains, and artists help them to do so. Don't disregard your chains; don't ignore them—use them to get stronger. Work in "relation" to your chains. A dancer's jump is notable because it's *against* gravity.

I remember taking a trip to the border between Mexico and the United States in El Paso, Texas. A border patrolman took me on a ride while he looked for people trying to get across the border. The routine was, he caught them, put them in jail, they were released from jail, they would get sent back to Mexico, they would come across the border again—he would find them again and bring them back to jail. Some of them expected to get caught. They went out every night and tried to get across, in order to get better at it. I tell this story not to make any comment one way or the other about immigration. I make it to say that every day you go into the studio, and every day that I try to learn a new interview, we are trying to defy certain realities.

As a visual artist, you are trying to break the chains that have to do with light and form and color. I am trying to break a chain that is a reality. The character is the character, and I am me. I am not the character—the best I can do is to try to get across the border, while the border patrol is not looking.

Our chains are a real part of our craft. But always, our passion must be greater than the chains.

ADS
Austin, Texas

Suicide and Keeping the Faith

Dear BZ:

I am so sorry to hear about the suicides at your school. Were they close friends of yours? Two in two weeks. How are you?

So teachers aren't discussing this as much as you would like. Schools have "liability issues." Yes. We are sometimes slaves to the law that was meant to protect us.

I am told that the problem of suicide among the young has reached epidemic proportions. You tell me that you feel alienated, that others around you feel alienated, and you have often asked me about the alienation of the artist. Is this the alienation of a generation? What's the cause? You can find out by opening up to others around you. One sure way to avoid alienation is to have the courage to break the barriers between you and others. To become a leader in the quest for intimacy—for real engagement. To have the strength again to share yourself with someone else, in the hope that it will be reciprocal. It is not always reciprocal. Not every interaction will bear fruit. I'm not talking about engaging only with people you like, or who are like you. I'm talking about real interaction, across all kinds of boundaries. What do you know, for example, about the janitors/janitresses in your school? Do they have children? Have you asked to see their pictures? What do you know, really know, about your teachers? Are they all human to you? The world is a community of human beings—all available for some degree of discourse, even if you get only a grunt.

I know this advice does not begin to touch on the tragedy in front of you. It is a time for learning and contemplation, and, if you wish, prayer and meditation. It's also one of those times when, traditionally, we go to the expressive arts for healing. Some suggestions: Listen to Schubert's String Quintet in C Major, D. 956; listen to the songs of Mary J. Blige; look at the paintings of Mark Rothko, or look at a sunset; read Carson McCullers's *The Heart Is a Lonely Hunter* if you haven't. Read James Baldwin's book of stories *Going to Meet the Man*, and in particular "Sonny's Blues."

Most important, think of all the times in the history of mankind that the banner of struggle and the light of hope have prevailed.

> Hope and optimism are different. Optimism tends to be based on the notion that there's enough evidence out there that allows us to believe things are gonna be better, much more rational, deeply secular, whereas hope looks at the evidence and says, "It doesn't look good at all. It doesn't look good at all. Gonna go beyond the evidence to create new possibilities based on visions that become contagious to allow people to engage in heroic actions always against the odds, no guarantee whatsoever." That's hope. I'm a prisoner of hope though. Gonna die a prisoner of hope.
>
> —*Cornel West, scholar*

ADS
San Francisco
May 2000

Stamina, Diamonds, and "Try"

Dear BZ:

I'm under the gun, preparing for a show I'll be doing to benefit education at the Museum of Modern Art. Nothing is as agonizing as learning lines. It's terrifying every time. I am *always* under the gun when it comes to learning lines. Not enough sleep. Not enough staff.

I think of three things:

1) A guy in a bar in San Francisco, downtown on Post Street, 1975. A nothing bar. I was drinking apricot brandy. He was a strange guy, older than me, looked like he hung out in bars a lot. He came over to where I was sitting with friends and said, "You have stamina, kid." Stamina. It matters. I don't know how he knew that.

2) A slogan I got from a swim coach: "A diamond is a lump of coal that stuck with it." Put that on your mental bulletin board. Sticking with it is slightly different from just plain stamina because it involves faith, having faith.

3) I'm thinking about Brent Williams, the rodeo bull rider who talks about "try." When he rides, he rides with "try." "Try" has a lot of stamina, but it also has a lot of heart. I think "try" is even better than stamina. "Ride the bull

with all the try you got." That could go on your mental bulletin board, too.

ADS
Sandra Cameron Rehearsal Studio
New York City
October 2003

Alienation

Dear BZ:

You ask whether an artist is inevitably alienated. The answer is no. I say that because I don't think we should romanticize alienation.

In writing to me you have often referred to loneliness or alienation. I've not yet addressed this directly. I've tried to keep most of my letters to you focused on practical things, but I should have listened more carefully, or read your remarks more carefully. Perhaps it will become a theme in your work.

I'm in Venice at the biannual festival of the arts. Despite the unbearable heat at the moment, I like Venice. I like the water; I like the thought that someone was imaginative enough to build a city around canals. Moving from place to place on foot or on water is fascinating. You can only go but so fast. I love the sound of all the human voices bouncing off of the stone streets and the large stone buildings, and the way multiple sounds of voices and music bounce around the large piazzas, especially around the Piazza San Marco.

It's a very emotional place.

Yet with all the throngs of people, all the parties and festivities, and all the beautiful aspects of the city, I am nonetheless aware of the alienation of many artists. It's very competitive here, for one.

Cautiously, I admit to you that some of my best work

has been created in moments of my life when I was experiencing an excruciating sense—almost an unbearable sense—of aloneness. A sense of being left, a sense of being an island, off, floating away at sea, with no hope of finding the shore, no human wave in sight.

You once asked me about a passage in Rainer Maria Rilke's *Letters to a Young Poet*: "How we squander our hours of pain. How we gaze upon them into the bitter duration to see if they have an end. Though they are really our winter-enduring foliage, our dark evergreen, one season in our inner year, not only a season in time, but our place and settlement, foundation and soil and home."

When you asked me if I had read Rilke, and if our letters were in the tradition of Rilke's *Letters to a Young Poet*, I should not have just shrugged off Rilke the way I did, so glibly. Here is what I wrote at the time:

"I have not read Rilke, and so I suppose I'm not in that tradition. The only thing I honestly know about Rilke is that when my acting coach had a fight with her aging mother, and sent a quote from Rilke to console her, her mother wrote back, 'And as for Rilke, I say crap on Rilke.' " I made light of what you were asking me. I hid behind humor and ignorance. Which wasn't fair.

The fact is, yes, pain *is* a soil. It is not the only soil for art. Pain *can* be very powerful. It can be productive. At the risk of sounding corny or old-fashioned, I maintain that even as we have pain to express, or even joy, the mode of expression is what you must build. What good does it do to have gasoline without a car (and vice versa)? Well, I suppose you could sell the gasoline to someone who had a car, but you won't find many buyers for your pure, unformed pain. The harsh reality about audiences is that *they care about your pain only if it helps them relieve or understand their pain.*

Do you know that in the nineteenth century (and probably before) there were doctors who gave themselves diseases and operated on themselves or their families? This was not, of course, for the sake of experiencing illness and pain, but for the sake of finding a cure. But similarly, as artists we can tolerate, for a while, great discomfort in order to explore discomfort: to explore it, you see, as a doctor might explore pain as the signal of something going on somewhere in the body.

In our schools we don't explore pain enough. I've written to you before about Maxine Greene, who studies, among other things, aesthetic education. She once quoted Herman Melville to me, in order to explain how art gets at those things that we cannot otherwise express. Here is what she said:

"At the beginning of *Moby-Dick*, Ishmael says, 'It is a damp, drizzly November in my soul.' There's no way of translating that into official language, but it opens for me so many parts of myself that I think I know myself a little better. Then he says, 'whenever I find myself involuntarily pausing before coffin warehouses, and bringing up the rear of every funeral I meet . . . then, I account it high time to get to sea as soon as I can.' He means it's time to open my imagination and go someplace I've never been."

Sometimes melancholy, longing, pain, or sadness can be a journey to something else. They can be a part of an inner mourning process that helps you leave a part of your life behind so that you can go on to the next phase.

They say that sanity is always determined in relationship to societal norms. And it's those people who can adjust to the insanity of the world—even who accept the insanity and the sickness of the world—who are called sane. Should we artists align ourselves with the sane, or shall we take a chance, and walk with our pain, or the pain of others—in order to tell their stories perhaps—to let them know that someone understands? To let them know that someone could imagine it, that someone could imagine what it would be like to look "wrong" when you have such sweetness and beauty inside, or even the opposite, that you look "right" on the outside and have such dissonance and even torment on the inside?

I am suggesting, BZ, that you see your pain with its integrity. I am not saying that you should accept it, or dwell or indulge in it; I am saying you should see it, just as you see the sunrise or the sunset. Your pain can be a source, like the color blue, or orange, for that matter. It can be one of your colors; it can be a tool.

In one very dark hour of my life, I wrote a play that people thought was important. So I won't deny that pain is a part of what we work with.

ADS
Venice, Italy
July 2003

Failure

Dear BZ:

Don't feel so bad about not winning the competition. I know how much it must hurt, but you'll learn over time not to take it so hard. Not that I think it ever gets easy. But there are so many competitions in front of you to win and to lose. (And you know what I think of that word *competition* anyway.)

First of all, there's no real failure if you're trying hard. Truly. Second, if there is failure, we can learn from it. Sometimes we try very hard and we fail, at least by our own standards. We may have made mistakes, and the "failure" shows these mistakes in the light of day; our failures illuminate new ways of doing things.

One of the more moving moments of my career was when I didn't get a Tony award. I was nominated for two, and winning one was what I needed to keep my show running on Broadway.

First a little background. My father was never very involved in my work in the theater. My mother came to everything I did. Not my father. I have a clear memory of my first piano recital. I was so nervous about what my father would think. The printed program did not have the name of one of the songs I was going to have to play, so this meant I would have to announce the name of the song before playing it. The hall was, at the time, to me, a sort of largish place. I'm sure it wouldn't seem so now. I got up to announce the name of my second piece, and I was so frightened and unsure of myself that I convinced myself that I couldn't remember the name of the song. This is odd, as I think back on it: As a kid, I had a very good memory, and as I told you, according to my mother, I always got cast in school "programs" because I could learn and remember my "parts." So why was it that in this case I couldn't remember the name of the song? Anyway, I couldn't. Having observed that people often garbled their words, and that it's unlikely that anyone in an audience will say out loud, "Say that again," I deliberately garbled my words. The whole time I was playing, I was worried about what my father thought about that. It was as if he were standing right over the piano.

Imagine my surprise when I learned that my father had not been in the hall at all, that he had chosen to stand *outside* the hall.

Now, as it turned out, this was not something that was specific to that occasion. Years later, I had my first New York success. In fact, it was my first national success: my play *Fires in the Mirror*. My father came to one performance on a Sunday afternoon, and didn't say much about what he thought. My little nephew talked throughout the performance and no one told him to be quiet. (Mind you, when I was a kid, if I so much as whimpered in church, my mother would whisk me out so as to not disturb the service.) I got used to the fact that my father had difficulty seeing my work, or congratulating me for it. When this show closed in New York, my mother came up to New York for the last show, and brought my father along. Would you believe that he chose to sit outside the theater, in the lobby? Just as he had done for my first piano recital? I did the last speech of that play, which is a father grieving the loss of his son, in honor of my brother and my father. I was performing *for* my father. I learned afterward my father wasn't there to hear it.

At a small party after the show, the artistic director of the theater came to me and told me that she had been very surprised to see my father in the lobby of the theater while the performance was going on. She told me that she had offered him a seat. The show was sold out, but she had said, "Mr. Smith, we'll find you a seat." And she told me he said, "Well, I've been falling asleep at my friends' funerals. I don't want to come inside; I'd be afraid I'd fall asleep." I assumed that he was simply not interested, or that at the very least he was unable to "be with me" in this work that I do.

Now, the Tony awards. Awards season starts way before the awards. (And that's true not just of the Tonys; it's true for a lot of these awards.) Awards can mean a lot in terms of your sense of achievement personally—but what they really influence is sales. (So our sense of achievement can be connected to our ability to sell if we're not careful.) Your value in the market is only if you sell. So it's like horse races. Your agents and all the people around you bank on these awards. And the whole thing winds up in an almost hysterical pitch.

Once the awards season starts, the newspapers start projecting who's going to win or not going to win, the Pulitzer Prize and the Tony awards being the most significant. (No one bets on Obies or the others.) One morning I was on my way to the gym and I made the mistake of looking at a column in the *New York Times*. On Saturdays I would always do a very thorough workout because I had two shows to get through and wanted to build stamina and energy. This particular column, written by Bruce Weber in the arts section, said something to the effect that there "wasn't much out there" for the Pulitzer that year. This column went on to say that there's nothing out there, because 1) they may not accept Tony Kushner's play, which was the second part of *Angels in America*, as a separate play, and 2) as for Anna Deavere Smith, "let's face it" (this isn't a direct quote but it was another one of those let's-face-it-sounding things), "she didn't write a word of it." Well! I was amazed. I had used the very same method a year before in my other plays and been a runner-up for the prize. It was clear that the status quo was not only not going to accept the innovation of what I do; they were going to try to make it look like I did something *wrong*! What worse thing could you say about an author than that they didn't write their words? It's plagiarism. Now, of course I don't write the words per se, and I put a sign up at the beginning of the show that says that the words are spoken by others. I credit all the speakers. However, the "writing" is in the construction of the "play." Apparently, for every person who thinks you've invented something new, there's someone else who doesn't see its value. At the suggestion of my publicist, I called Bruce Weber and ranted and railed about the unfortunate use of the words "didn't write a word of it." I regretted that call. I was overly emotional, and probably came off looking like a stark raving maniac. (I've since had lunch with Mr. Weber. He's a terrific guy.)

Worse was my discovery that one of the journalists on the prize committee had said my intention had been that I and only I could perform my work. Nothing could be further from the truth. In fact I've created my work in *particular* for people like your classmates, BZ, to perform! See how worked up I still get?

The Tony awards were very important for the survival of my show. In my case—as is the case with many people who have shows on Broadway—if your show is having financial trouble, sometimes a Tony award is the only thing that can save it. My agent had said he wasn't going to come to the awards, because the tickets to the ceremony were $1,000; he'd just be at the party afterward. That should have been an indication right then and there. My date, at the time a congressman and formerly the head of the NAACP, Kweisi Mfume, had been listening to comments in the bathroom when he came to see the show. He said something like, "Well, we'll see if they're ready for you. If they're progressive you have a chance. If not . . ." That was another indication. So I did not get either Tony that I was nominated for, and the party that followed was more painful than not. This was clearly, then, the end of my Broadway run.

I got home to my apartment (where everything felt very "real"—back to a previous letter when you asked me the difference between art and reality), and there was a message from my father waiting for me on my voice mail. It surprised me that it was my father, and not my mother. By now, my father was seventy-five years old. It was actually a little less than a year before he died. And he said (I wish I still had the message), he said in a low voice, "I know you must be disappointed. But don't take it too hard." That really broke my heart.

"Don't take it too hard." Because in the way he said "Don't take it too hard," I could feel his resignation about his failures in his own life. And perhaps life is all about aspirations on the one hand and resignation on the other. It was the kindest thing my father had ever done. Much more moving than, for example, the time I had a victory to report—my having achieved tenure at Stanford University. "I'm really proud of you," he had said. The first time he'd ever said that. And certainly that should have felt like an achievement to me. But more important was the tone of his voice when he said, "Don't take it too hard."

So, in that spirit I say to you, "Don't take it too hard."

ADS

Faith

Dear BZ:

"I have fought the good fight,
I have finished the race, I have kept the faith."
—II TIMOTHY 4:7

No doubt about it, more important than the race and the fight is faith. Whatever that means, spiritual or otherwise. It's crucial to keep the faith. Never stop believing.

Faith requires discipline and a lot of imagination.

ADS
Baltimore, Maryland
September 2003

art and society

The Place for Art

Dear BZ:

You all have just been informed that the school's painting studio will be shut down and turned into a biology lab? And just days before the Christmas holidays? This is horrible news.

All right. First of all, it does no good to disparage the sciences. I do not agree with your arguments about biology and how few people will actually use it when they get out of school. That's ridiculous. Some people do make use of biology, and frankly, more need to. You need to organize your thoughts and come up with sound arguments that respect the basic ideas of what education is meant to be. Rather than saying something to devalue science, look to history and other cultures to find examples of how art has been a pivotal part of culture and of history, and of civilization. (Remember that when the World Trade Center was attacked, artists of all kinds were asked to participate in the many different ceremonies, vigils, etc. They were a key part of the healing process. The building of the new site could not happen without aesthetics and an understanding of aesthetics.) The awareness of the importance of the artist's vision always needs to be enhanced in schools. It is shocking to me that the argument continually needs to be made—but it does. And now is the time for you to practice building the most surgically elegant, magnificently informed arguments you can.

Knowledge of any kind cannot be valued only in terms of

its use. We can't say that the poetry of the Renaissance is going to do a doctor any good, because we don't know if that's true. And for that matter, it's the same line of thinking that eliminates the painting studio. I am sure that those in power see little need for painting in the practical lives you all may lead.

Put up a fight! It may not stop the studio from being shut down, but you must use the moment to alert everyone in the school community of what it means to lose this part of your school. You also need to practice fighting. Develop your muscles; you will need them in the future. Don't make the fight about the worth (or not) of what is going to go on in the biology lab. It's not either/or. It's not winner take all. Maybe there's a solution that allows both the lab and the studio to exist. There's always the possibility that those coming up with the current "solution" to the space problem have not been as imaginative as they could have been. Have you spoken with the arts faculty in the school? See what you can learn from them about the battle that has been waged so far.

It would be ideal if all schools, all cities, all countries had beautiful studio spaces, concert halls, dance spaces, theaters. By the way, all schools, all cities, all countries don't have good biology labs either, or good hospitals or health care centers, for that matter.

The fact is, the fight for a space for the expressive arts is always a battle. That battle has to do with the value of the work we do in the marketplace. But we can't "market" process, or we don't. What I'm saying is, it's hard enough to find a place for a ballet company to perform; what's harder is to find the places where ballet dancers are trained—and in your case, where painters are trained. And this training, especially good training, is more often in the private sector than in public schools. You are right: The notion that the studio should be in the basement of the school is appalling—no natural light. Do biologists need natural light? I don't know. There is, as you know, a growing desire in the country among leaders in politics and industry as well as education to strengthen math and science in the schools. There's nothing wrong with that; in fact, it's important. As artists, however, young artists, you can take up the banner and argue that spaces for both the sciences and the expressive arts must exist.

Never forget that your outside position has a number of disadvantages, but it also has a number of advantages. Often people think of artists as a little "out there" in every way, and don't consider them a part of the grown-up discussion at the table. Your school has had a "grown-up discussion" without you and determined to get rid of the studio. It's time now for you and other artists, and your friends (I would choose some young biologists, by the way) to show that you have a grown-up argument and a grown-up solution about where on school property you can find proper space and proper light to do your work.

Make an argument to someone in the community, outside of the school, who might have the financial resources to help. If the request for the money were initiated by students, it could be very powerful.

The artist is often making the argument for his or her existence and for his or her presence. This is true in democracies, and brutally true in regimes and governments that clamp down on expression. Even in a democracy, certain kinds of ideas, certain kinds of art are allowed to flourish, and others are not—depending on the market for those ideas, those works of art.

Schubert's brilliant Quintet D 956 was not appreciated until after his death. We could fill an enormous archive with many such examples all over the world. By nature the artist sees something that others do not see.

Now for some tough love. You should be saying something that is not yet expressed in any other means. You really can't just "express" for the sake of expression and expect others to engage with you—or, for that matter, care about you. To get your space, you must *instigate* the engagement. Finding a place for the arts comes second to finding that which you are trying to say. It may be that at your school, as artists you have not yet felt the need to "say" anything. Now's your opportunity. What is it in the community of your school that is not evident, not expressed? Quite apart from the current situation of your studio, what is going on in your school that is not expressed at the moment? Give expression to that. You will become evident. And even if you are painting outside or doing watercolors—keep working. The more timely and elegant and necessary your expression, the more evident it is that you need a place to be—a place where others can come and find you, at work.

ADS
Carmelo, Uruguay
December 21, 2003

Taking Care of Yourself

Dear BZ:

I'm sitting on a floor, taking a break, in one of the most gorgeous dance studios I have ever been in in my life. Marcos, an assistant from a couple of years ago, and a former student, is helping me learn lines for the movie of my play *Twilight*, which will begin shooting in a week or so. Marcos has gone down to get us some juice and coffee. I've rented this studio at the San Francisco Ballet to prepare for the movie—that is, to prepare the acting part of it. We've been working in here for about a week.

The light coming into this room is perfect. The room is huge and immaculate. The dance studios at Juilliard, in New York, are pretty spectacular, but they are nothing like this. There are locker rooms outside for the students. It's so quiet and peaceful. No one's here. The school's not in session.

When I arrived today, there was a very attractive man dancing. I thought I had disturbed a rehearsal.

"I'm sorry," I said. I barged in with my bags full of fifty tape recordings. I use tape recordings in order to study the voices of the characters I'm learning, plus my tape recorder, plus my video camera, which I use during rehearsal to video the work and then watch it back.

"It's fine. It's fine," he said jovially. "I was just messing around."

He started putting his things away as I got set up.

"Are you with the San Francisco Ballet?" I asked.

"Oh, no, no." He laughed. "I haven't danced in years. I used to, long ago." He was in great shape, so I couldn't imagine it was that long ago.

"Are you a choreographer?" I asked. I thought maybe he had his own dance company and, like me, had rented the studio.

"Oh, no," he said. "I'm the company doctor."

"Is someone ill?"

"No. The company has a full-time doctor. . . ."

"On call?" I asked.

"No, I'm full-time staff." He said all of this in an easy, breezy way.

"The ballet has a full-time, year-round doctor, like, every day?"

"Yes," he said.

"Wow!" I said.

"Have a great rehearsal," he said, and left.

Wow! A full-time doctor, and this gorgeous space. There are certain kinds of artists, and certain kinds of art, *that are taken care of*. Others are not. Money, patronage, philanthropy go for that which is established. It is very, very rare that philanthropy puts money into the daily care of things that are truly off center—in this country. (Not in other countries. I think of William Forsythe's Frankfurt Ballet. And here there are some exceptions: Robert Wilson would be an exception.) It would be wonderful if we were all taken care of that way. But we aren't. We live in a prince-and-pauper world. Some artists are in an area of art that is fully endowed. Others are not. That's a fact.

Even if you are not cared for, you have to take care of

yourself. Your health is important. The idea of the starving artist who ultimately ends up cutting his ear off is an idea I have rarely seen played out. In most circles of successful artists, there is a lot more health and wholesomeness than one is led to believe. You need rest; you need good nutrition for your body, your mind, and your soul. You need lots of ideas and a brain and nervous system that can absorb them. Think of your imagination as a muscle that needs to be plump with health. Stay hydrated.

ADS
San Francisco
May 1999

Fame and Authenticity

Dear BZ:

For my twenty-first birthday, a friend carved the following quote into a simple piece of wood: "Fame is a vapor, riches take wings. Only one thing endures—character."

This is true. Yet we now live in a celebrity culture. As George Stephanopoulos, one of President Clinton's right-hand men, said to me in an interview, "We live in a celebrity culture, and the president is the celebrity in chief."

It's all around us. I can't pooh-pooh fame. The fact is, if you happen to become well-known, it gives you access and resources that you might not otherwise have. We live in a media age—and more people have become and will become famous. Fame means only that you are exposed—that you are on a stage that may be a national stage or an international stage. As the world gets smaller, we will know about more and more people.

The one word of caution is not to confuse fame with authenticity. That is to say as you regard the fame of others, and in the event that you become famous, many of the things we have talked about here come into play and are magnified. It keeps coming back to the fact that even if the world audience authorizes you as one of "them"—wants to embrace your work—you must still remain the author. In other words, don't believe the hype. Even if it's about you.

Shine on.

Anna

Fool

Dear BZ:

As an artist, I see myself as one of the clowns, one of the fools, one of those who see the world upside down and inside out. I am a fool in the classic sense. But I take my foolishness very seriously.

ADS
Washington, D.C.
The day after Martin Luther King's birthday, 2004

the death of cool

Urgency

Dear BZ:

I just got back from seeing the hip-hop performer Common. Wow.

He had such urgency when he came out on the stage. It taught me something. It's simple. Don't even bother coming out onstage—or doing anything in the realm of artistic communication—if you don't have a sense of urgency.

Nothing cool here.

ADS
Los Angeles
March 2003

The Death of Cool

Dear BZ:

Freezing cold today in New York. Just before Christmas. And the streets of New York have their share of the holiday spirit. The entire fall has been festive. The whole fall has felt like a holiday. New York is just bursting at the seams with art, art, art. So much energy and so much art! And this city is the city where it can all happen. It has the wealth to support it, but it also has many young artists like yourself, who have come here, as always, in droves, living in the boroughs or wherever, and with whomever they can pay the rent, to drink in all this city has to offer at a very dynamic time in its history and to give back their talent. We more than survived September 11; we are *thriving*. As the year comes to an end, you can feel the energy of conversation and engagement in restaurants, in galleries, in concert halls, in shops. People come here to engage. People come here not just to be seen but to see. It's a real people city. It is a city where art is sold and it is a city where art is made. You may or may not find nurturers here—but if you come here with friends you can nurture one another. This is just about the best relationship between artists and arts supporters that you can find anywhere in the nation. It doesn't mean it's easy. You have to be tough, you have to be resilient, you have to have a lot of stamina, a lot of energy, and a lot of guts. But if you have those things in any proportion this is a magnificent place to be at the moment. I simply cannot be cool about New York. It is a hot town. And it heats me up! Even on a relentlessly unforgiving, freezing cold day like today.

Wynton Marsalis, the fantastic trumpet player and composer, has just unveiled Jazz at Lincoln Center—two theaters and a jazz club right in the center of New York City at Columbus Circle—the view out of one of the theaters is down Central Park South. It's incredible. And just a few blocks away, the Alvin Ailey American Dance Theater has opened the largest facility devoted exclusively to dance in the United States. Both of these groups were started by and are run by African Americans. Alvin Ailey, who has been dead for several years now, may have imagined it—but he may not have believed it could happen. One of his most steadfast dancers, a man called Masazuma Chaya, now the associate artistic director of the Alvin Ailey American Dance Theater—once told me, "Alvin always said he will never be on the front page of the *New York Times*, unless he died." And apparently, that was the case. When he died, it was announced on the front page. But his legacy lives. One of his great ballets, *Revelations*, has been endowed so that it can be performed *forever.* Can you imagine? People endow buildings, and universities, and hospital wings—but a ballet? A dance? A live performance?

I say all this to give you a context of a moment that we are in—now in the arts in New York City. The Museum of Modern Art has opened a new building that is exciting and architecturally wonderful.

Today I had lunch with Wynton Marsalis at a Japanese restaurant in Midtown. Over sushi and warm sake we talked about the blues. "The blues is *everything.*" And we talked about relationships—and how we take what we inherit in our families out onto the streets and then back into the families we create.

"I've been thinking about Miles Davis, and the birth of cool," I said. (Miles Davis did a famous album called *Birth of the Cool.*) Wynton nodded as he scooped up a piece of sea urchin.

"I've been thinking about this idea," I said hesitantly, "this idea of the death of cool."

"It's time for it to be dead," he said emphatically.

I was relieved. It's always hard when you are in one art form, and you are trying to find a place to connect with someone of a different art form and a different language.

"So—what's cool?" I asked.

"Miles was the epitome of cool," he said. "Lemme tell you something," he said, taking a quick look around and moving his head in closer over the table. "Every time I saw Miles, he'd say, 'If you see Cicely tell her I said hi.' Or he'd say, 'How's Cicely?' [Cicely Tyson was the ex-wife of Miles Davis.]

"And *then*," he said, shaking his head, "the way he wrote about her in his book!" He shook his finger like that was a big no-no. "Naw. That's not right. That was cold."

I hadn't read the book—but I know from what others have told me that the book would make it look as though it was a bitter relationship.

"Cool is . . . cool is you don't show emotion. Cool is you never raise your voice. Miles never raised his voice." Wynton shook his head. "He would talk real soft. The idea is you keep all your emotion inside in everyday life and you don't let it out till you play." He shook his forefinger again, and took another sip of warm sake.

"Miles told me one time, he said, 'The only answer to a question is no.' Just no."

Right. So it's time for cool to die.

So the death of cool . . . would do what? It would probably bring more tones, more color, more emotion, more love, more raw spirit, more argument, more energy. More authenticity? More compassion? More laughter? More tears? More open hearts?

Try it. Be uncool. As uncool as you can possibly be. Write to me about the result.

Be hot.

ADS
New York City
Christmastime 2004

You'll End Up Like Dostoevsky

Hi, BZ:

I'm by the sea. I spoke with my friend Michael, with whom I bonded in acting school. We've been soul mates ever since those days of doing scenes together. There's nothing like an arts education. You learn so much from the people you collaborate with, about their lives, about what makes them tick. He learned a lot then about how my heart had been broken by a love affair gone wrong, and here I was years later, telling a similar tale. In the midst of our talk, I told him that even though the romance was over, I was pleased that I had written a couple of pretty good poems.

"I have to say, at least I wrote a couple of good poems out of all this pain."

"Watch out or you'll end up like Dostoevsky."

"What do you mean?"

"You know those Russians—they were always suffering."

There is an idea that artists suffer—and that their suffering brings good work. This is true and not true. The great scholar Cornel West tells me that despair is something that is a reach for the great artist. I don't think he means indulgence; I think he means the capacity to empathize at a deep level. It may just be that such empathy requires, in fact, a degree of mental health. On the other hand there's no denying that some great artists do and did, in fact, suffer in reality. Ironically, some of the greatest comics were in the greatest amount of personal pain.

And so I began to think about Dostoevsky and what it would mean to "end up like Dostoevsky." I asked Paul VanDeCarr, who helps me on all of my projects, and who studied Russian literature, "Did Dostoevsky suffer for his art?"

Here's what he wrote me back:

> I don't know that Dostoevsky's suffering "necessarily" made him a better novelist. Or that it "necessarily" allowed him access to certain realms of human experience. After all, not everyone who suffers is an artist, much less a great artist, or even lets their suffering make them more compassionate or more fully human, if that's the right way of putting it. But I guess your question, in part, at least in Dostoevsky's case, is not whether his suffering made him a great artist, but whether his art required that he suffer. Am I on the right track here?
>
> In Dostoevsky's case, I think he was endowed with a great mind, he worked hard on his art, and he was part of a historical tradition, or a history—this huge, great country that for hundreds of years was in frequent and grand strife, conflict, and war (most significantly with Napoleon, most recently to Dostoevsky's own time). So their literary tradition—including Dostoevsky's writing—grows partly out of that history, too.
>
> There's also the question of suffering "for" one's art. Not just whether suffering helps produce great art, but whether the actual creation of the art is itself a source of suffering—since the process of birthing art is or can be difficult, painful. Which in turn might then spawn more great art. Dostoevsky saw himself as suffering for his art in both senses. Dostoevsky had a romantic vision of

> his own suffering—it's a tradition that goes a long way back, as you know. In Russian literature, and in Dostoevsky's case specifically, this is very much informed by Christian views on suffering in order to usher great art/creation into the world. I think Dostoevsky scholars will tell you basically the same thing.

I find this response very useful. Suffering in and of itself will not produce great art—we can see that Dostoevsky was endowed with a great mind and that he was part of a historical tradition that helped augment what he had already.

I believe in joy as a source for great work, and try to enjoy my work as much as I can. At the same time, I think that as people who are able to stand inside and outside of a situation, we should not attempt to escape pain. Great ecstasy is as difficult to bear as pain. That occurred to me early one summer when I jumped into Lake Tahoe. It was freezing, but so clear and so unbearably beautiful that I thought I'd choke from joy.

Our discipline is to search for and reach all the extremes of the human experience. For that we must live *in* the world, not only in our own biographies. We must keep our eyes and hearts open to the world and its challenges.

Deciding to become an actress was not easy. I was bothered by two things. One problem I inherited from my grandmother, who was a devout Christian. She thought of actors and dancers as "sinful." When I was in acting school, she sent me a letter written in what was, by then, a scrawl—she was ill, and probably had a form of Alzheimer's. The letter read: "I hear you want to become an actress. Please don't take off your clothes. Here's five dollars; buy yourself a new dress." And there was a five-dollar bill inside. The letter was both moving and liberating. My grandmother had been a true soul mate, and she was seeing her final days. Yet the letter helped me see that I was *afraid* of acting (and I wonder, BZ, if any of your fears—fears you've written to me about—have their origin in family attitudes), because I had been given messages by those whom I respected that this was a *dangerous*, *unclean* life. My second problem was that I also had the notion that to play a drug addict, for example, I had to experience what a drug addict experienced. I was very relieved to discover that metaphor and empathy could replace experience.

In addition to empathy—and taking yourself to the "place" of pain—is the sheer joy of knowing that you can do what your art form calls for you to do—that you have the skills, that you have the technique. All those blues singers and opera singers, when asked if they go to the place of the pain in the song, will tell you that they are just trying to hit the note. I had the extreme pleasure of sitting next to William Forsythe, director of the Frankfurt Ballet, at a dinner. I asked him how he became a choreographer. He said it had its roots in high school, and it was very simple: "'Cause I could *dance*." He went on to say how much he loves being in the studio. "To me, dancing is like *eating*," he said.

You can look to the history of artists and imagine yourself as one who suffers alone in a heatless garret with torn gloves and water dripping out of a single spigot. But you also will find in those histories healthy lives, with their share of pains and joys—just like in other professions. It might not be as dramatic or as romantic to go for the latter—but it's an option.

Doctors do not have to get the diseases they treat. Stockbrokers don't always make all the money they handle either.

The baker does not eat all the cakes he bakes. The great mystics don't live all the scenes they see. Neither do prophets.

"Have a rich life and haiku will come"—that's what my mime teacher told me when I first started studying acting, and I've been trying hard to make that the case. Still working on it!

ADS
Montauk, New York
December 2004

The World Is Your Lab

Dear BZ:

I am in San Francisco, where I became an artist: Where I learned the special discipline of making things out of mind, body, spirit. I am overlooking the glorious San Francisco Bay, the Bay Bridge, and the hills of Marin County. It is Sunday morning. I have been watching the day emerge since five A.M. Now there are a few boats on the bay. I can see Alcatraz, which was a prison. To my right are very tall buildings. I am on the forty-second floor, in a hotel. Outside of the hotel, police and fire trucks have surrounded the streets. The bellman who brings me the paper talks at length, wondering about why this is so. He is in his late twenties and looks to be part Asian and part white. He has an accent. I am unable to discern what kind. "Today is the anniversary of the 1906 earthquake," he announces.

I marvel at this. He hands me the *San Francisco Chronicle* and the Sunday *New York Times*. The cover of the *New York Times* bears a photograph of several men. They look shocked. Their hands are waving in the air. They are all focused on something that is not in the picture. The hands of one of them are covered in blood. The caption reads, *Palestinians Surrounded the Car in Which the New Hamas Leader, Dr. Abdel Aziz Rantisi, Was Killed Yesterday*. To the left, an article is headlined, *Pre-9/11 Panel Shows Warnings More Dire and Persistent*. In the middle, *U.S. Troops Shut Long Sections of*

Two Main Routes to Baghdad, and another, *Three U.N. Police Die in Shootout at Kosovo Jail*. And so on. Oddly, under the fold of the cover there is another photograph of another group of people with their hands up, their mouths open, impassioned, crying out. The caption reads, *About Five Hundred Worshippers, Many from Ghana, Filled the Church of the Pentecost in the Bronx on Palm Sunday*. And to the right, *How I Spent Summer Vacation: Going to Get into College Camp*. Something else catches my eye. *The Underside of Fashion—A Class Action Suit Charging Modeling Agencies with Price-Fixing Unveils an Underside of New York's Fashion Business.*

This is our world.

That is, this is our world in literate, middle-class, educated, cosmopolitan America.

Now the light has moved and the buildings outside my window are bright and shining. The light and the white of the buildings, the pastels of the buildings in this city, make it one of the most beautiful cities in the world.

Every time I come here it is as if I have returned home to my roots. This feels more like my roots than Baltimore, where I was born and grew up. In fact, as I walk these streets the memories and the feelings are more powerful, more complex than I have in the home of my natural birth. It is as if I were reborn when I came here, in my twenties. I was reborn, I was revolutionized, my eyes were unveiled, my heart was opened, my legs were freed to dance rather than walk, my spirit was awakened. Every time I return I am filled with a feeling of hope and promise and a wish: a wish to be in union with this physical beauty and with the political heritage of the place. I often wish I could go back in time and meet up with the history of this place.

I pick up the paper again. Each world is different. "An Israeli helicopter strike on Saturday . . ." What is the world inside the helicopter? "Two American women working as prison guards with the United Nations in Kosovo were killed Saturday, and ten other Americans and an Australian working as prison officers were wounded when a . . ." Another world.

BZ, you can visit worlds. You can tour the world. Not with the army, not with the airlines, but with your curiosity. You are responsible for your itinerary.

BZ, you make the time, you find the time, you create the structure. It is a freedom and a responsibility. The world is your lab. The canvas is the report. Or the dance floor, or the sheet music, or the computer, or the film.

The world is the lab; the world is the substance. How much of the world can you absorb?

We have access to know everything about one another, and yet we know little.

You have an invisible badge of freedom, an invisible passport that says, "Go—move, gather, be bold, be brave, see, take, absorb." Make new words, make new images, new sounds, new alliances.

As an artist you are a student of the human condition. There is no syllabus. You can go to school and seek some structures, some techniques, some advice. Ultimately you must make your own course description, you must discover your own book list, you must make your own regimen, your own discipline. You can work as hard as you like. Or not. You can use the time or not. You can use the world—as much or as little as you like.

There is a crisis in the world right now. As humans will we bring ourselves together, or tear ourselves apart? Will we protect natural resources or further deplete them? Will technology dominate the human spirit or is the human spirit indomitable?

There are lawyers, doctors, inventors, businesspeople, soldiers, thieves, preachers, pimps, murderers, lovers of children, abusers of children, lovers of wives, abusers of wives, lovers of husbands, abusers of husbands, those who would like to construct new ideas of family, those who are bound to old ideas.

Your job is not defined. There is no bar exam for you to pass; there is no oath for you to take. Nonetheless you have a large responsibility and possibility if you would like to take it.

As artists we cannot afford to hide out in our tiny rooms. We must expand our capacity to absorb. And we should use our "passports" to go, metaphorically, where others might go.

The old model of educating artists was to create a "safe space" in which they could be "nurtured." That was the model of how I was trained. But the nurturing did not happen for everyone. Many of us found our own way. And I'd venture to say that when I look back, I've heard less in the long run from my old classmates who were "nurtured" than I have from those who cut their own path, took a chance, worried less about safety and ventured forth because they had no option.

As you go on this journey, BZ, I cannot promise safety. I can try to help bring you to a kind of artistic leadership. And that calls not for safety, but resilience, and breaking the molds when you can. It calls for absorbing this fractious world, absorbing it, sifting through it in your dreams, in your subconscious, in less than obvious ways, and giving it back to a viewer or an audience so that they see the cover of the newspaper differently.

Here's my big question to you and your generation of artists. It's a question that comes because we are now so very entrenched in a celebrity culture. Are you becoming an artist because you want the world to look at *you*? Or are you becoming an artist because you would like to use your ability to attract attention—and the ability to get people to look at your work—in order to cause them to see themselves and the world differently *through* you?

The celebrity culture is turning in on itself. Now is the time to take the other path. Use your ability to see things upside down and inside out to cause those around you to do the same. It might help them consider another route than the popular route. The less popular route needs exploration.

We are students of the human condition, with our own course of study. The time is yours. Take it. Use it wisely.

The dawn has completed its course. It's day now. I can't tell if it will be beautiful or not. There are two small boats that I can see, and a few cars are going across the wonderful red stripe that crosses from San Francisco to Marin—the long red stripe being the Golden Gate Bridge.

Till later,

ADS
San Francisco
April 2004

The Ultimate Presence

Dear BZ:

Bonita Bradley, my first yoga teacher, is in Thailand. She called me from there, and I could not call her back with the number she left me. In the meantime, we all got news of the tsunami that struck Southeast Asia. Needless to say I was very worried.

Finally I found her, with her daughter's help, safe and sound in a guesthouse. She had been visiting a monastery in Thailand and had been doing very long meditations with the monks. When she told me about the experience of being at the monastery, she told me a story that represents the ultimate presence.

Bonita knows a lot about the body, and has mentored me throughout my career. She's been studying and teaching how the body and the imagination "click," or work together. We are all "bodies" of knowledge. The more in tune we are, the more we are connected—inside and outside. The more in tune we are spiritually and environmentally, the more whole we are, and the more this is revealed in our bodies. Bonita said, for example, that Thai women are very connected to their sexuality—not in the way that we see people broadcasting sexuality as commerce on the fronts of magazine covers, but in the way they move and walk, the way they are *inside* and out. Americans, according to Bonita, are very disconnected from their bodies.

We are told that the animals knew that the tsunami was coming. Mankind has disconnected itself from the earth. We look to technology to connect us. In some ways we can see technology as an extension of our humanness, but in another way we can, and do, overrely on it. We are even disconnected from the very technology we create.

As tragic as the tsunami was, it barely rested in our consciousness before it was removed from the covers of newspapers to be replaced by the story of Brad Pitt and Jennifer Aniston's breakup. Is that a tragedy, too? It has taken up more space in the media than the tsunami.

Bonita and I spoke just a few days after Christmas, and I think of this image as one of the nicest Christmas presents I've gotten in a long time.

Here's the scene:

A very simple meditation room in a very rural village in northern Thailand. It was at the end of the meditation. The monk walked over to the middle of the room and stretched his arm up to turn the lightbulb that was hanging from the ceiling. That simple gesture of turning the lightbulb filled the room. His entire body aligned to do that gesture. It was like the movement of a dancer. That's what Bonita described to me, so in this case, art and reality meet, BZ. The aesthetic meets the everyday!

The monks eat only what is given to them by the people in the village. In return for the food they are given, the person gets a blessing from the monk. Bonita was walking through the village one morning, and she came upon the monk who had adjusted the lightbulb in the meditation room. She handed him an apple. He smiled at her, and the smile was the blessing.

I asked her what the blessing felt like. She said that the smile of the monk filled her with a feeling of well-being, a feeling of well-being that she experienced all day. That simple smile had such power.

What is presence? What is its purpose? What is art? What is its purpose? It might sound too simple to say that your presence has the potential to fill a room, an audience, a town, a gallery with a feeling of well-being. It is as simple as the turning of a lightbulb—but it comes from being in tune with where you are and what you are doing. Such presence can bring messages of goodwill, and it can also bring warnings of troubles to come. Presence is your ability to both absorb the world around you by being fully in its presence, with all that is beautiful, troubling, and mundane. It is your ability to absorb and to transmit what you have absorbed, with the simplest of gestures. Through discipline, you can learn how to absorb the complex and to translate it simply.

Be present in the world, BZ. It's been my great pleasure to have written to you for these few years.

Stay strong, stay new, stay you,

ADS

APPENDIX: RESOURCES FOR YOUNG ARTISTS

NATIONAL ENDOWMENT FOR THE ARTS—**www.nea.gov.** **NEA,** 1100 Pennsylvania Ave., NW, Washington, D.C. 20506. Phone: 202-682-5400. E-mail: **webmgr@arts.endow.gov.** Has a resource listing on their Web site broken down by discipline available at **www.nea.gov/resources/disciplines/index.html.** Disciplines include Arts Learning, Dance, Design, Film/TV/Radio/New Media, Folk and Traditional Arts, Literature, Local Arts Agencies, Multidisciplinary Arts, Museums, Music, Musical Theater, Opera, Presenting, Theater, Visual Arts. Within each of these categories are listings for artists of color. FROM THE WEB SITE: "The National Endowment for the Arts is a public agency dedicated to supporting excellence in the arts, both new and established; bringing the arts to all Americans; and providing leadership in arts education. Established by Congress in 1965 as an independent agency of the federal government, the endowment is the nation's largest annual funder of the arts, bringing great art to all fifty states, including rural areas, inner cities, and military bases."

YOUR STATE OR REGIONAL ARTS AGENCY—Look up your state or regional arts agency at **www.nea.gov/partner/state/SAA_RAO_list.html.** Each of these agencies has a Web site, and extensive listings for artists and arts organizations in all disciplines, including those specific to young artists, artists of color, LGBT artists, etc. For complete listing, see page 211.

COMMUNITY ARTS NETWORK—**www.communityarts.net.** The Community Arts Network (CAN) promotes information exchange, research, and critical dialogue within the field of community-based arts. The Web site is managed by Art in the Public Interest. They publish a regular e-newsletter called *API News*, available at **www.communityarts.net/api/apinews.php.** They also have a reading room that you can browse according to discipline or by subject, available at **www.communityarts.net/readingroom/readingroom.php.** One of the subjects is Arts and Youth, an extensive listing of youth arts resources, available at **www.communityarts.net/readingroom/resyoulinks.php.**

NYFA SOURCE—**www.nyfa.org/nyfa_source.asp?id=47&fid=1.** New York Foundation for the Arts, 155 Avenue of the Americas, 14th Floor, New York, NY 10013-1507. Phone: 212-366-6900. E-mail: **NYFAweb@nyfa.org.** Sponsored by the New York Foundation for the Arts, NYFA Source is the most extensive national directory of awards, services, and publications for artists. Listings include more than 3,400 arts organizations, 2,800 award programs, 3,100 service programs, and 900 publications for individual artists across the country. More programs are added every day. Database is searchable by ethnicity, LGBT, age, etc.

FOUNDATION CENTER—**http://fdncenter.org/.** Has searchable database of grants. Basic info search is free, but full search requires subscription. However, the Foundation Center has libraries in New York and San Francisco, where you can do complete searches for free. Offices and/or libraries available in cities nationwide, where you can conduct free complete funding searches, and take workshops. Offices in Atlanta, Cleveland, New York, San Francisco, and Washington D.C. Addresses and Web sites for each follow:

ATLANTA: 50 Hurt Plaza, Suite 150, Atlanta, GA 30303
Tel: 404-880-0094, Fax: 404-880-0087
http://fdncenter.org/atlanta/

CLEVELAND: 1422 Euclid Avenue,
Suite 1600, Cleveland, OH 44115-2001
Tel: 216-861-1934, Fax: 216-861-1936
http://fdncenter.org/cleveland/

NEW YORK: 79 Fifth Avenue, New York, NY 10003
Tel: 212-620-4230, Fax: 212-691-1828
http://fdncenter.org/newyork/

SAN FRANCISCO: 312 Sutter Street,
#606, San Francisco, CA 94108-4323
Tel: 415-397-0902, Fax: 415-397-7670
http://fdncenter.org/sanfrancisco/

WASHINGTON, D.C.: 1627 K Street, NW,
3rd Floor, Washington, DC 20006-1708
Tel: 202-331-1400, Fax: 202-331-1739
http://fdncenter.org/washington/

FROM THE WEB SITE: "The Foundation Center's mission is to strengthen the nonprofit sector by advancing knowledge about U.S. philanthropy. To achieve our mission, we: • Collect, organize, and communicate information on U.S. philanthropy. • Conduct and facilitate research on trends in the field. • Provide education and training on the grant-seeking process. • Ensure public access to information and services through our Web site, print and electronic publications, five library/learning centers, and a national network of cooperating collections. Founded in 1956, the center is the nation's leading authority on philanthropy and is dedicated to serving grant seekers, grant makers, researchers, policy makers, the media, and the general public."

ALTERNATE ROOTS—**www.alternateroots.org.** E-mail: **info@alternateroots.org.** Alternate ROOTS, 1083 Austin Ave. NE, Atlanta, GA 30307. Phone: 404-577-1079, Fax: 404-577-7991, Toll free: 1-888-871-9898. For Southeastern artists. Mission is to support the creation and presentation of original art that is rooted in a particular community of place, tradition, or spirit. FROM THE WEB SITE: "As cultural workers we strive to be allies in the elimination of all forms of oppression. ROOTS is committed to social and economic justice and the protection of the natural world, and addresses these concerns through its programs and services."

BREAKTHROUGH—**www.breakthrough.tv.** Breakthrough is an international human rights organization that uses media, education, and popular culture to promote values of dignity, equality, and justice. It has affiliate offices in the United States and India.

Breakthrough USA: 24-36 85 Street,
Jackson Heights, NY 11372
Tel: 718-457-4300, Fax: 718-457-4307

Breakthrough India: A1/133 Safdarjang Enclave,
New Delhi 110029
Tel: 91-11-2617-6181 Fax: 91-11-2617-6185

INSTITUTE ON THE ARTS AND CIVIC DIALOGUE—**www.artsandcivicdialogue.org.** The institute was founded to foster the creation of works of art that deal with social change and to enhance civic engagement. It was founded by Anna Deavere Smith.

STATE, REGIONAL, AND JURISDICTIONAL ART AGENCIES

This list is available at **www.nea.gov/partner/state/SAA_RAO_list.html.** For the Web site for any of these organizations, click on the organization name when on the Web site. Or just type in "www" followed by the domain name listed in the e-mail address. The domain name is what comes after the "@" symbol in an e-mail address. For example, if the e-mail address is **general@artsmidwest.org,** then the Web site address is **www.arts midwest.org.**

National Assembly of State Arts Agencies
1029 Vermont Avenue, N.W., 2nd Floor
Washington, DC 20005
202-347-6352
nasaa@nasaa-arts.org

REGIONAL ARTS ORGANIZATIONS

U.S. Regional Arts Organizations Web Site
http://www.usregionalarts.org

Arts Midwest
2908 Hennepin Avenue, Suite 200
Minneapolis, MN 55408-1954
612-341-0755

TT/Voice: 612-341-0901
general@artsmidwest.org

Mid-America Arts Alliance
912 Baltimore Avenue, Suite 700
Kansas City, MO 64105
816-421-1388
info@maaa.org

Mid-Atlantic Arts Foundation
201 North Charles Street, #401
Baltimore, MD 21202
410-539-6656
TT: 410-539-4241
maaf@midatlanticarts.org

New England Foundation for the Arts
145 Tremont Street, 7th Floor
Boston, MA 02111
617-951-0010
info@nefa.org

Southern Arts Federation
1800 Peachtree Street, Suite 808
Atlanta, GA 30309
404-874-7244
TT: 404-876-6240
saf@southarts.org

Western States Arts Federation
1743 Wazee Street, Suite 300
Denver, CO 80202
303-629-1166
staff@westaf.org

STATE AND JURISDICTIONAL ARTS AGENCIES

Alabama State Council on the Arts
201 Monroe Street
Montgomery, AL 36130-1800
334-242-4076
TT/Relay: 1-800-548-2546
staff@arts.state.al.us

Alaska State Council on the Arts
411 West 4th Avenue, Suite 1E
Anchorage, AK 99501-2343
907-269-6610
TT/Relay AK: 1-800-770-8973
asca_info@eed.state.ak.us

American Samoa Council on Arts, Culture & Humanities
P.O. Box 1540
Pago Pago, American Samoa 96799
011-684-633-4347

Arizona Commission on the Arts
417 West Roosevelt
Phoenix, AZ 85003
602-255-5882
general@ArizonaArts.org

Arkansas Arts Council
1500 Tower Building
323 Center Street, #1500
Little Rock, AR 72201
501-324-9766
info@arkansasarts.com

California Arts Council
1300 I Street, #930
Sacramento, CA 95814
916-322-6555
TT: 916-322-6569
cac@cwo.com

Colorado Council on the Arts
1380 Lawrence Street, Suite 1200
Denver, CO 80204
303-894-2617
TT: 303-894-2664
coloarts@state.ca.us

Connecticut Commission on Culture and Tourism
One Financial Plaza, 755 Main Street
Hartford, CT 06103
860-256-2800
artsinfo@ctarts.org

Delaware Division of the Arts
State Office Building
820 North French Street
Wilmington, DE 19801
302-577-8278 (from New Castle County)
302-739-5304 (from Kent or Sussex Counties)
TT/Relay: 1-800-232-5460
dclarts@state.de.us

District of Columbia Commission on the Arts & Humanities
410 8th Street, NW
Washington, DC 20004
202-724-5613
TT: 202-727-3148
cah@dc.gov

Division of Cultural Affairs
Florida Department of State
1001 DeSoto Park Drive
Tallahassee, FL 32301
850-245-6492
TT: 904-488-5779
info@florida-arts.org

Georgia Council for the Arts
260 14th Street, Suite 401
Atlanta, GA 3031
404-685-2787
gaarts@gaarts.org

Guam Council on the Arts & Humanities
Office of the Governor
P.O. Box 2950
Tiyan, GU 96932-2950
011-671-475-2242
arts@ns.gov.nu

State Foundation on Culture & the Arts
250 South Hotel Street, 2nd Floor
Honolulu, HI 96813
808-586-0300
TTD: 808-586-0740
sfca@sfca.state.hi.us

Idaho Commission on the Arts
2410 North Old Penitentiary Road
Boise, Idaho 83712
208-334-2119
info@ica.state.id.us

Illinois Arts Council
State of Illinois Center
100 West Randolph, Suite 10-500
Chicago, IL 60601
312-814-6750
TT: 312-814-4831
info@arts.state.il.us

Indiana Arts Commission
150 West Market Street, #618
Indianapolis, IN 46204
317-232-1268
TTD: 317-233-3001
IndianaArtsCommission@iac.in.gov

Iowa Arts Council
600 East Locust
State Capitol Complex
Des Moines, IA 50319
515-281-4451

Kansas Arts Commission
Jayhawk Tower
700 SW Jackson, Suite 1004
Topeka, KS 66603
785-296-3335
TT/Relay: 1-800-766-3777
KAC@arts.state.ks.us

Kentucky Arts Council
300 West Broadway
Frankfort, KY 40601-1980
502-564-3757
kyarts@ky.gov

Division of the Arts
Louisiana Department of Culture, Recreation, & Tourism
1051 North 3rd Street
P.O. Box 44247
Baton Rouge, LA 70804
225-342-8180
arts@crt.state.la.us

Maine Arts Commission
193 State Street
25 State House Station
Augusta, ME 04333
207-287-2724
TT: 207-287-5613
MaineArts.info@maine.gov

Maryland State Arts Council
175 West Ostend, Suite E
Baltimore, MD 21230
410-767-6555
410-333-4519 (TDD)

Massachusetts Cultural Council
10 St. James Avenue, 3rd Floor
Boston, MA 02116-3803
617-727-3668
TT: 617-338-9153
web@art.state.ma.us

Michigan Council for Arts and Cultural Affairs
702 West Kalamazoo
P.O. Box 30705
Lansing, MI 48909-8205
517-241-4011
artsinfo@michigan.gov

Minnesota State Arts Board
Park Square Court, Suite 200
400 Sibley Street
St. Paul, MN 55101
651-215-1600
800-8MN-ARTS
TT/Relay: 612-297-5353
msab@arts.state.mn.us

Mississippi Arts Commission
239 North Lamar Street, Suite 207
Jackson, MS 39201
601-359-6030

Missouri Arts Council
Wainwright Office Complex
111 North Seventh Street, Suite 105
St. Louis, MO 63101-2188
314-340-6845
oarts@ded.mo.gov

Montana Arts Council
316 North Park Avenue, Suite 252
Helena, MT 59620-2201
406-444-6430
TT/Relay: 1-800-833-8503
mac@state.mt.us

Nebraska Arts Council
The Joslyn Castle Carriage House
3838 Davenport Street
Omaha, NE 68131-2329
402-595-2122
TT/Voice: 402-595-2122

Nevada Arts Council
716 North Carson Street, Suite A
Carson City, NV 89701
775-687-6680
jcounsil@clan.lib.nv.us

New Hampshire State Council on the Arts
2 1/2 Beacon Street
Concord, NH 03301-4974
603-271-2789
TT/Relay: 1-800-735-2964

New Jersey State Council on the Arts
225 West State Street
P.O. Box 306
Trenton, NJ 08625-0306
609-292-6130
TT: 609-633-1186
njsca@arts.sos.state.nj.us

New Mexico Arts
P.O. Box 1450
Santa Fe, NM 87504
505-827-6490
TT: 505-827-6925

New York State Council on the Arts
175 Varick, 3rd Floor
New York, NY 10014
212-627-4455
TT: 212-387-7049

North Carolina Arts Council
Department of Cultural Resources
Raleigh, NC 27699-4632
919-733-2111
ncarts@ncmail.net

North Dakota Council on the Arts
1600 East Century Avenue, Suite 6
Bismarck, ND 58503-0649
701-328-7590
comserv@state.nd.us

Commonwealth Council for Arts & Culture
P.O. Box 553, CHRB
CNMI Convention Center
Commonwealth of the Northern Mariana Islands
Saipan, MP 96950
9-011-670-322-9982

Ohio Arts Council
727 East Main Street
Columbus, OH 43205-1796
614-466-2613
TT/Relay: 1-800-750-0750
webmaster@oac.state.oh.us

Oklahoma Arts Council
P.O. Box 52001-2001
Oklahoma City, OK 73152-2001
405-521-2931

Oregon Arts Commission
775 Summer Street, NE, Suite 200
Salem, OR 97310
503-986-0082
TT: 503-378-3772
oregon.artscomm@State.OR.US

Commonwealth of Pennsylvania Council on the Arts
Finance Building, Room 216A
Harrisburg, PA 17120
717-787-6883
TT/Relay: 800-654-5984

Instituto de Cultura Puertorriqueña
Apartado 9024184
San Juan, Puerto Rico 00902-4184
787-724-0700

Rhode Island State Council on the Arts
83 Park Street, 6th Floor
Providence, RI 02903-1037
401-222-3880
TT: 401-277-3880
info@risca.state.ri.us

South Carolina Arts Commission
1800 Gervais Street
Columbia, SC 29201
803-734-8696
jguinn@arts.state.sc.us

South Dakota Arts Council
Office of Arts
800 Governors Drive
Pierre, SD 57501-2294
605-773-3131
TT/Relay: 1-800-622-1770
sdac@state.sd.us

Tennessee Arts Commission
Citizens Plaza
401 Charlotte Avenue
Nashville, TN 37243-0780
615-741-1701
rich.boyd@state.tn.us

Texas Commission on the Arts
P.O. Box 13406
Austin, TX 78711-3406
512-463-5535
TTY: 512-475-3327
front.desk@arts.state.tx.us

Utah Arts Council
617 East South Temple Street
Salt Lake City, UT 84102
801-236-7555

Vermont Arts Council
136 State Street
Montpelier, VT 05633-6001
802-828-3291
TT/Relay: 800-253-0191
info@vermontartscouncil.org

Virginia Commission for the Arts
223 Governor Street
Richmond, VA 23219
804-225-3132
TT: 804-225-3132
arts@arts.virginia.gov

Virgin Islands Council on the Arts
41-42 Norre Gade, 2nd Floor
P.O. Box 103
St. Thomas, VI 00802
340-774-5984

Washington State Arts Commission
711 Capitol Way S., Suite 600
P.O. Box 42675
Olympia, WA 98504-2675
360-753-3860
TT/Relay: 206-554-7400 or 1-800-833-6388
info@arts.wa.gov

Arts & Humanities Section
West Virginia Division of Culture & History
1900 Kanawha Boulevard East
Capitol Complex
Charleston, WV 25305-0300
304-558-0220
TT: 304-348-0220

Wisconsin Arts Board
101 East Wilson Street, 1st Floor
Madison, WI 53702
608-266-0190
TT: 608-267-9629
artsboard@arts.state.wi.us

Wyoming Arts Council
2320 Capitol Avenue
Cheyenne, WY 82002
307-777-7742
TT: 307-777-5964
ebratt@state.wy.us

ACKNOWLEDGMENTS

My thanks go to my editor LuAnn Walther, to my agent Gloria Loomis, to John Siciliano and Marla Jea at Anchor Books, and to George Shepherd.

Thanks also to all my students since the first time I stepped into a classroom, and to my muses Amory Houghton Jr. and Priscilla Dewey Houghton.

ILLUSTRATION CREDITS

Photograph of Memphis by Mary Ellen Mark.

Jacob Lawrence, *The Migration of the Negro #15*, 1940–41, © 2005 The Estate of Gwendolyn Knight Lawrence/Artists Rights Society (ARS), New York. Courtesy of The Phillips Collection, Washington, D.C.

Photograph of Naomi Campbell by Patrick Demarchelier for *Harper's Bazaar*.

Photograph of Brent Williams by Diana Walker.

Photograph of Anna Deavere Smith by Diana Walker.

Pablo Picasso, *Guernica*, 1937, © 2005 Estate of Pablo Picasso/ Artists Rights Society (ARS), New York. Photo credit: John Bigelow Taylor/Art Resource, New York.

Paul Cézanne, *The Bather*, ca. 1885. Lillie P. Bliss Collection (1.1934). Digital Image © The Museum of Modern Art/ Licensed by SCALA/Art Resource, New York.

Lyle Ashton Harris, *Memoirs of Hadrian #17*. Monochromatic dye diffusion transfer print (Polaroid), 24 x 20". Courtesy of CRG Gallery, New York.

ALSO BY ANNA DEAVERE SMITH

HOUSE ARREST AND PIANO
Two Plays

In *House Arrest*, Smith examines the relationships between a succession of American presidents and their observers from Clinton and Monica Lewinsky to Jefferson and Sally Hemings. In *Piano*, she follows the tangled lines of race, sex, and exploitation in a prosperous Cuban household on the eve of the Spanish-American War.

Drama/1-4000-3357-8

TALK TO ME
Travels in Media and Politics

Anna Deavere Smith sets out to discern the essence of America by listening to its people and trying to capture its politics. She travels to locations that range from presidential conventions to a women's prison in Maryland. Memoir, social commentary, and meditation on language, *Talk to Me* is as ambitious as it is compellingly unique.

Drama/0-385-72174-9

FIRES IN THE MIRROR
Crown Heights, Brooklyn, and Other Identities

In August 1991, simmering hostilities in the racially polarized neighborhood of Crown Heights, Brooklyn, exploded after an African-American boy was killed by a car in a rabbi's motorcade and a Jewish student was slain in retaliation. Derived from interviews with people who experienced or observed the Crown Heights riots, *Fires in the Mirror* is an extraordinary portrayal of ethnic turmoil.

Drama/0-385-47014-2

TWILIGHT: LOS ANGELES, 1992

Twilight: Los Angeles, 1992 is Anna Deavere Smith's haunting work of "documentary theater" in which she uses the exact words of people who experienced the Los Angeles riots to expose and explore the devastating human impact of that event.

Drama/0-385-47376-1